Strike for America

The Jacobin series features short interrogations of politics, economics, and culture from a socialist perspective, as an avenue to radical political practice. The books offer critical analysis and engagement with the history and ideas of the Left in an accessible format.

The series is a collaboration between Verso Books and *Jacobin* magazine, which is published quarterly in print and online at jacobinmag.com.

Other titles in this series available from Verso Books:

Playing the Whore by Melissa Gira Grant
Utopia or Bust by Benjamin Kunkel

Strike for America

Chicago Teachers Against Austerity

by
MICAH UETRICHT

VERSO
London • New York

First published by Verso 2014
© Micah Uetricht 2014

1 3 5 7 9 10 8 6 4 2

Verso
UK: 6 Meard Street, London W1F 0EG
US: 20 Jay Street, Suite 1010, Brooklyn, NY 11201
www.versobooks.com

Verso is the imprint of New Left Books

ISBN-13: 978-1-78168-325-5
eISBN-13: 978-1-78168-326-2 (US)
eISBN-13: 978-1-78168-639-3 (UK)

British Library Cataloguing in Publication Data
A catalogue record for this book is available from the British Library

Library of Congress Cataloging-in-Publication Data
A catalog record for this book is available from the Library of Congress

Typeset in Fournier MT by Hewer Text UK, Ltd, Edinburgh, Scotland
Printed in the US by Maple Press

CONTENTS

INTRODUCTION

On June 7, 2012, there were two visions of teacher unionism on display in Chicago. One could be found in a hotel overlooking the Chicago River, rubbing shoulders with the city's and the world's elites downtown; the other in public schools throughout the city.

Randi Weingarten, president of the American Federation of Teachers (AFT), had flown into Chicago to speak at the Clinton Global Initiative, an annual event held by former President Bill Clinton's foundation. She was to sit on a two-person panel, moderated by militant centrist Fareed Zakaria, to discuss the recently announced Chicago Infrastructure Trust, an infrastructure development program that allows corporations to invest in and profit from financing of public infrastructure projects for things like sewers, roads, and water lines. Her copanelist was Mayor Rahm Emanuel.

Weingarten sat next to the mayor, politely chuckling at jokes made by a man who had declared war on public school teachers and all but announced his intentions to disassemble public education in the city of Chicago. She praised

Emanuel's public-private partnerships in infrastructure development, making no mention of his plan to dramatically expand Chicago's charter schools—a public-private partnership par excellence—intended to slip the free market's foot in the door of public education before completely privatizing it. Nor did she speak of the months during which the mayor antagonized the city's education workforce, his attempts to rescind contractually obligated raises for the teachers, or the major battle teachers were locked into with the mayor over the future of public education in the city.

At precisely the same time, Chicago teachers were in their schools—not teaching, but voting on whether or not they would strike during their contract negotiations with the mayor. They had no words of praise for Emanuel's public-private partnerships or his vision for education reform in Chicago, which they identified as harmful to both teachers and students. They were rebuking him in the strongest way they could: by voting to strike come the fall. Although school was not in session, 90 percent of all members of the Chicago Teachers Union (CTU) and 98 percent of those who voted called for a strike. Teachers on vacation were tracked down so that no vote would be lost; one teacher who was hospitalized and undergoing rehabilitation was even met at the hospital by a small group of CTU members to help her vote—an act, she explained in a video, that was critically important to her personally.

Weingarten never joined these teachers and never showed her face at a school where teachers were voting. After speaking alongside Mayor Emanuel, she flew out of Chicago. She would eventually join striking teachers on the picket line, after whatever behind-the-scenes attempts national union staff likely engaged in during the months leading up to the walk-off had failed. But, her belated presence notwithstanding, the strike, eventually touted as one of the most important labor victories in recent American history, was authorized almost without any acknowledgment from the president of the AFT.

In many ways, the contrast between the events at the high-
rise hotel and the crumbling neighborhood schools was indicative of the choice that teachers unions, and organized labor as a whole, face in the twenty-first century. Would they continue to opt for an insider strategy, praising the neoliberal politicians and titans of capital who wanted to destroy them, in the hope that perhaps, if they were sufficiently deferential, these forces would spare them and their members? Or would they confront those enemies and their ideologies head-on, with militant tactics like strikes and deep organizing within communities?

The extreme inequality in America's public school system has been both willfully ignored and a cause célèbre for crusading activists and wealthy philanthropists throughout the country's history. Today the trend favors philanthropists, who generally believe that the way to reform education is to privatize it. Education, once seen as a sacrosanct public institution, has become another public good to be dismantled and handed over to the marketplace. In some cities, this has meant the institution of voucher programs, which allow parents to take their children out of public schools, enroll them in private schools, and still receive public money to cover tuition. Elsewhere, public schools have been shuttered and teachers laid off. Nearly everywhere, teachers have been identified as the culprits behind schools' supposed poor performance.

   Perhaps most central to the education privatization agenda today is the growth of charter schools, which receive public money but are privately run and not held to many of the same benchmarks as public schools, providing a key path for free-market forces to enter the public education system. Their popularity has exploded in recent years: the number of American students enrolled in charters quadrupled from 1999–2000 to 2009–2010.[1] Public school closures have paved the way for charter expansion, as shuttered neighborhood schools are soon replaced by charters. The policy has led school districts like Chicago and New Orleans to close schools that are deemed to be "failing," much as an investment firm might choose to eliminate underperforming assets from its portfolio. The closures are often determined by scores on standardized tests, which have become central at all levels of education in the country as a metric determining which schools are worthy of preservation and which are not.

A privatized educational system will inevitably renege on many of the supposed foundational principles of public education: to educate all children in society regardless of who they are or where they come from, to develop critical

---

1 National Center for Education Statistics, "Charter School Enrollment," nces.ed.gov/fastfacts/display.asp?id=30.

thinking and provide a broadly humanistic education, and to do this creatively rather than just honing skills by rote teaching and joyless assessments like standardized testing. By ignoring these principles, whatever remnants of democratic control remain in the public schools will be eliminated. Schools will serve the purpose of training future workers to accumulate profits for future bosses.

Indeed, only a few years into the project of privatization, much of this has come to pass. Charter schools in Chicago, for example, currently accept roughly half the number of special education students that regular neighborhood schools enroll because such students require additional financial resources.[2] Poor and working-class children of color face the upheaval of moving to new schools when theirs are closed. There they may encounter young, inexperienced teachers who view teaching as a way station to future elite careers, not as a lifetime commitment. These students serve, in effect, as guinea pigs for new educational experiments, whereby every few years a new reform proposal to "fix" failing schools— but never to "fix" poverty—is adopted. Standardized testing has become a national obsession, with students even at the kindergarten level being forced to take a battery of such tests on nearly every subject, from reading and mathematics to physical education and art. The art of teaching at its best requires giving teachers the freedom to structure their lesson plans on the basis of their students' interests, to linger on a

---

2 Ben Joravsky, "Stacking the Odds in Favor of Charter Schools," *Chicago Reader*, April 13, 2011.

given subject that has unexpectedly piqued their students' curiosity, and to incorporate pedagogical methods other than those narrowly prescribed from above. All of these freedoms have been eroded to make room for drills for standardized tests.

Every Chicago public school has a democratically elected local school council made up of parents, community members, teachers, and an administrator, and these bodies have real decision-making power over basic school issues like choosing principals. At charters, this democratic mechanism has been eliminated. The resulting losses have included commitment to all students regardless of ability, long-term stability of teachers and schools, joy in learning, teachers' control of their work, democracy—all these have disappeared or been eroded as free market education reforms have advanced.

And schools shaped by the dictates of the market have failed on their own merits. Despite an obsession with standardized testing, for example, studies of charter schools repeatedly show that students at all levels do not, on the whole, outperform traditional public school students. An examination of charter school research conducted by the Brookings Institution in 2009 revealed that "none of the studies detects huge effects—either positive or negative" on students' educational achievements. (They do, however, often institute excessive disciplinary and student fine policies.[3] As education historian Diane Ravitch writes, "If

---

3   Ted Cox, "Charter Schools Ring Up Fines, More Public Funding," *DNAInfo*, January 2, 2013.

evidence mattered, most of these issues would not be at the top of our nation's education agenda. But no matter how many research studies or evaluations were produced, the corporate school reform movement pressed forward, unfazed.")[4]

The agenda to privatize public education and turn it into a market good requires an attack on teachers and their unions because no other body is as capable of amassing the resources necessary to fight such an agenda. And no other body has as big a stake in doing so, since the neoliberal attack on public schools necessarily includes whittling away at the pay, benefits, and on-the-job protections that teachers have won through struggle over the last century. Teachers' work has become structured by the same kinds of "lean production" methods as for-profit businesses, with teachers facing expanded classroom sizes, longer hours, and reduced or no planning periods. Charter school teachers in Chicago, almost all of whom are nonunion, make nearly $24,000 less, on average, than traditional public school teachers who are unionized. Teacher tenure protection is being weakened while merit pay is being introduced in school districts around the country.[5]

Chicago is no stranger to this agenda. Education policy scholar Pauline Lipman describes the city as "the incubator, test case, and model for the neoliberal urban education

---

4   Diane Ravitch, *The Death and Life of the Great American School System: How Testing and Choice Are Undermining Education*, Basic, 2010, pp. 275–76.

5   Will Johnson, "Lean Production," *Jacobin*, Fall 2012; Anastasia Ustinova, "Charter-School Growth Fuels Chicago Teacher Fears," *Bloomberg*, September 12, 2012.

agenda. Chicago is where big city mayors go to see how to restructure their school systems."[6] Chicago's public schools are under the complete control of the mayor, who appoints the school board and chief executive officer; there are no democratic mechanisms whereby citizens can play a role or remove those they deem incompetent or damaging. Mayor Richard M. Daley used this power in 2004 to push "Renaissance 2010," a program initially designed to close schools but later modified to "turn around" schools (which included firing a school's entire staff) it deemed "failing." Ninety-two schools in the city are "Ren2010" schools, and three quarters of them have been converted to charter schools.[7]

Before 2013, the city had closed seventy-five public schools over the previous twelve years under a variety of justifications ranging from underutilization to poor standardized test performance; 40 percent of those schools were reoccupied by privately operated charter schools. In the 2013 round of school closings—the largest in American history—the city moved to close forty-nine elementary schools and one high school program, nearly all of which served majority black students on the city's South and West sides. The expansion of charter schools, however, continues apace.[8]

Charters are the preferred vehicle for neoliberal education reform, in Chicago and elsewhere, because they allow private

6   Pauline Lipman, *The New Political Economy of Urban Education: Neoliberalism, Race, and the Right to the City*, Routledge, 2011, p. 19.

7   Becky Vevea, Linda Lutton, and Sarah Karp, "Map: 40 Percent of Closed Schools Now Privately Run," *Catalyst Chicago*, January 15, 2013, catalyst-chicago.org.

8   Ibid.

operators to receive public funding but avoid teachers unions or basic disclosure rules about how they spend that money. At the beginning of 2013, there were 110 charter schools in Chicago, nearly twice as many as in 2005. Chicago Public Schools funding for charter schools increases every year, growing from $482 million in 2013 to $570.5 million by 2014, when some 13 percent of CPS students will be attending charters. Only fourteen of those 110 charters were unionized as of mid-2013—which explains the nearly $24,000 gap in average annual pay between nonunion charter and unionized public school teachers' salaries as well as charter teachers' lack of basic workplace protections. Since the 2000s, the CTU's total membership has shrunk by several thousand owing to layoffs, while the nonunion teaching force has expanded.[9]

In addition to its dubious distinction as a central neoliberal testing ground, Chicago was also the birthplace of American teachers' unionism at the turn of the nineteenth century. It is fitting that a major challenge to the national education reform agenda would come from the CTU, fighting alongside communities bearing the brunt of the neoliberal agenda.

The last four decades in the Chicago Teachers Union saw nearly uninterrupted rule by one organization, the United Progressive Caucus (UPC). The UPC was formed in the 1970s as an amalgamation of racial justice caucuses in an

9   Ben Joravsky and Mick Dumke, "Public Schools, Private Budgets," *Chicago Reader*, July 21, 2011; "Chicago Public Schools Fiscal Year 2013 Amended Budget," cps.edu/fy13budget/pages/Schoolsandnetworks.aspx; Becky Vevea and Sarah Karp, "Mapping Chicago Public Schools Priorities," WBEZ, June 13, 2012; Ben Joravsky, "Fighting for the Right to Fire Bad Teachers—And Good Ones, Too," *Chicago Reader*, September 26, 2012.

effort to push a conservative union leadership unconcerned about the widespread racist treatment of both students and teachers. Between 1972, when the caucus first took power, and 1987, the UPC led the union out on strike five times. But by the 2000s, when the neoliberal education agenda was in full swing, the UPC leadership had grown complacent and reluctant to fight back. After a failed attempt at liberal reform in 2001, activist teachers formed a radical caucus, the Caucus of Rank-and-File Educators (CORE), to challenge the incumbent leadership; it to emphasized member engagement, direct action, partnership with community groups and other unions, and put forward its own progressive education reform agenda. The origins of that caucus were in organic teacher-community partnerships to oppose school closures and turnarounds in poor and gentrifying communities. Years of organizing and agitating eventually led to that caucus's victory—and with it a new organizing agenda to challenge the free market education consensus.

It was CORE's leadership that helped guide the union and its members to engage in a tactic that has become increasingly rare in the twenty-first-century labor movement: the September 2012 strike. Over 90 percent of all 26,000 teachers, clinicians, and paraprofessionals who make up the union voted to walk off the job. When the strike came, teachers were soon to be found everywhere one looked on Chicago's streets; the city's downtown was engulfed in a sea of red, the union's color, with tens of thousands of educators and their supporters shutting the city down for hours at a time. It was the most explicit and militant rebuke to the free market consensus on education reform in recent memory, undertaken by one of the largest unions in Chicago.

Said CTU organizer Matt Luskin several weeks after the strike,

> I don't think it is an overstatement to say that the overwhelming majority of CTU members really believe that this was a strike against the neoliberal corporate education reform agenda; really do believe this was a strike about the future of education in black and brown neighborhoods in particular, about the future of public education.[10]

The strike came at a time of rising anger against growing inequality and fiscal austerity. Early 2011 saw the occupation of the Wisconsin State Capitol in response to Governor Scott Walker's Budget Repair Bill, which gutted collective bargaining rights for public sector workers. The action was led not by union leadership but by unionized graduate students and other private and public-sector union members. Later in the year, a motley crew of mostly young activists responded to a call in *Adbusters* magazine and began Occupy Wall Street, capturing the public's attention for several months and bringing the plight of "the 99 percent" into the national discourse.

Both actions inspired people around the country. They gave voice to the widespread anger about the worsening objective conditions for everyone besides the ultrarich and

---

10 "Lessons of the Chicago Teachers Strike: Matthew Luskin." September 30, 2012, YouTube.

made American inequality a central topic of debate nationally. Neither, however, can list many concrete
accomplishments. The Wisconsin protests failed to beat back
Walker's bill—union leadership, constrained by the limits of
a bill passed by a Republican Party in control of all three
branches of Wisconsin state government, channeled the
momentum from the capitol into several uninspiring and ulti-
mately failed recall campaigns. For all its successes, Occupy
Wall Street, hampered in part by its anarchist roots, was
unable to articulate any clear demands on the state, much less
mobilize public support for a new program of reform.

Neither of these observations is intended to denigrate
either uprising; indeed, both played key roles in articulating
the rising tide of anger around inequality. But it was the CTU
strike that first identified that rising tide in the form of an
angry union membership and channeled it into an effective,
militant political form, winning real gains and building power
both for education workers and the communities they serve.
Tactics like building occupations, encampments, and other
street actions changed the national dialogue on the neoliberal
consensus; the CTU actually slowed the neoliberal project's
forward march, wrung some concessions out of it, and positioned itself to better lead fights against that project in the
future.

This kind of fight is uncommon for the major US teachers
unions, the National Education Association (NEA) and the
AFT (the CTU being a member of the latter), and the majority of their locals. The period of militant teacher unionism
around the Great Depression or amid the upsurges of the

1960s and 1970s—including illegal strikes, jailed leaders and occasional street battles—is a distant memory. Few teachers unions are legally permitted to strike during contract negotiations, and those few are rarely willing to strike, fearing that the tactic will be viewed as too alienating—indicating a lack of concern for affected students. Likewise, few teachers unions have created intimate relationships with students' parents and the communities where they teach, at times using their unions more like insurance companies with which they occasionally file claims rather than as organizations aimed at advancing mutually beneficial struggles.

And few leaders of teachers unions are willing to push back against free market education reformers. Some are comfortable publicly expressing distaste for their more zealous adherents, like former Washington, DC, Public Schools Chancellor Michelle Rhee, but not many take on the "vulture philanthropists" at large foundations like the Walton or Gates Foundations or liberals in the Democratic Party championing their agenda. Even fewer have put forward their own vision for what progressive education reform should look like, linking a strong critique of free market reform with their own proposals to shore up education as a public good.

Much of organized labor finds itself in a position similar to that of the national teachers unions—afraid to engage in industrial action or even viewing the strike as an outdated relic—without clear principles guiding what a positive agenda for changing society could look like. Instead, it sticks to a timid insider strategy, hoping to wait out the storm that has decimated so much of the movement over the last four decades while utilizing top-down organizing techniques that do not engage broad sections of its membership and ignore the world of workers and communities outside its own union.

This "business unionism" has a long history in American labor. Since its birth in the mid-nineteenth century, American labor's leadership has fought against demands for broad-based organizations that address concerns of wider swaths of the working class; it has opposed more leftist politics in favor of a conservative agenda and narrow mission.[11] This style of unionism is suicidal. During a time of austerity in particular, it is unable to succeed even on its own parochial terms of delivering better pay and benefits to its members. That is made clear by the declining living standards over the past four decades of even the unionized American working class.

The CTU opted instead for a more militant unionism with close ties to communities to build a broad educational justice movement in Chicago—"social movement unionism." Unlike business unionism, which views unions' power as coming from their officers' ability to negotiate and win concessions, the CTU's style of unionism sees its power as coming from its members as well as other unions and communities outside the union. For the CTU, that has meant a democratic, bottom-up organizing style that engages the entirety of the union's membership; it has also meant widespread coalition building with organized communities

---

11   Paul Buhle, *Taking Care of Business: Samuel Gompers, George Meany, Lane Kirkland, and the Tragedy of American Labor*, Monthly Review, 1999.

throughout Chicago. The CTU's program under CORE offers an example of what a fighting left-unionism, rather than the kind of centrist unionism so prevalent throughout American labor history, can look like in a time of austerity. And although it is far too early to tell whether the union's victories are harbingers of a genuine radical politics triumphing over the centrism of recent decades, the possibility that the CTU might blaze such a trail does exist.

The American labor movement is in shambles, teetering on the brink of extinction. The CTU, meanwhile, can be credited with a major defeat against a powerful neoliberal mayor, a newly energized and mobilized membership, and a setback for the free market education agenda. If other sections of the labor movement were to take some cues from the CTU about militant, bottom-up, democratic left-unionism, unions' extinction might become less of a certainty.

1

CORE

When the slate put forward by the Caucus of Rank-and-File Educators (CORE) won the 2010 election for the leadership of the Chicago Teachers Union (CTU), it made few headlines. Some Chicago media covered it, as did a few prescient bloggers, but most ignored it. Stories about labor get short shrift in the mainstream press these days, and stories about internal union battles are almost entirely off the radar. But if local journalists had examined the 2010 CTU leadership election closely they would have realized that, in many ways, a referendum on two starkly different visions of teacher unionism by Chicago's 26,000 educators had just taken place.

There was the incumbent United Progressive Caucus (UPC), which had little to say about school closures in poor neighborhoods of color, attacks on teachers, and the advance of free market education reform. While its early roots were in rank-and-file racial justice caucuses within the union, by 2010 the UPC leadership had long atrophied. They paid themselves massive salaries and pensions, used expense accounts questionably, and were entrenched enough to fend off challengers. Down from its once-lofty ambitions, the old guard came to represent a stale top-down business unionism. And there was CORE—rooted in an organic community-teacher coalition against school closures, a broad left politics, and an uncompromisingly combative and democratic union-ism whose raison d'être was in a perceived need to end union capitulation to neoliberal education reform.

The rise of CORE indicated not only a leftward shift in Chicago teachers unionism but also a rejection of a labor model that mandated progressivism from on high. CORE was born out of rank-and-file struggles against unresponsive, regressive leadership; immediately upon taking power, CORE began working to train its members to lead the way in the union. Without CORE's victory, the 2012 Chicago teach-ers strike would never have come to pass and Chicago teachers unionism would not have appeared on the national radar as a model for struggle. In two years, the caucus's left-wing leadership built on relationships with community organizations that had been years in the making to mobilize in support of its strike. It assembled an incredibly efficient organizing apparatus centered around identifying activist teachers, giving them leadership and organizing training, and having them organize every single teacher in their schools. It formed formal and informal relationships with other organ-izing campaigns throughout the city, tying the teachers' visions for education reform to broader campaigns for social justice.

At a time when teachers and their unions find themselves under assault, the story of CORE offers some practical lessons for how teachers can take over their unions to defend public education and how radical democratic unionism of all types can spread.

Chicago is the birthplace of American teacher unionism. The multiple unions that existed in the early 1900s and eventually merged in 1937 to become the CTU were forerunners of teacher unionism throughout the country. The city has also been home to activism by rank-and-file teachers dissatisfied with their union's leadership on issues ranging from general education reform, to pay and benefits, to racial inequity between white teachers and teachers of color. During the Great Depression, for example, after repeated attempts to engage union leadership to help garner months of back pay owed to Chicago teachers by the Board of Education, high school teacher John M. Fewkes led mass demonstrations through the city's downtown—which included the ransacking of multiple banks and pitched street battles with teachers hurling textbooks at mounted police. Teachers were soon given the back pay owed them.[1]

In the 1960s, progressive white teachers formed Teachers for Radical Change in Education, emboldened by the radical climate at the time and dissatisfied with the union leadership's lack of action on racial justice and educational inequity. At the same time, multiple independent African American teacher organizations were formed to pressure leadership to

---

1   John F. Lyons, *Teachers and Reform: Chicago Public Education, 1929–70*, University of Illinois, 2008, pp. 38–42.

advance a broadly progressive agenda and defend black teachers—they included the Black Teachers Caucus and the Teachers Committee for Quality Education. Among their grievances was the fact that the union refused to campaign for the full certification of "full-time basis substitutes" (FTBs)—an almost entirely black group of teachers who worked for years as substitutes because of the racist tests and evaluations required for full certification. These teachers were junior members of the union without full voting rights; they therefore organized a group called Concerned FTBs. After a 1968 FTB strike, which the CTU leadership had officially opposed and begged Concerned FTBs leaders not to go through with, the CTU eventually prodded the Illinois State Legislature into action to allow a path for FTBs to become regular teachers.[2]

These independent efforts have always terrified union leadership. Men's Teachers Union President C. L. Vestal wrote in a 1932 letter that "the leaders of the teacher organizations wish to do their part to keep our common boat on an even keel in spite of the storm, but the rank and file are becoming even harder to quiet. . . . They are putting more and more pressure on their leaders to 'do something.'"[3]

The union thus has a long history of rank-and-file members battling calcified, conservative leadership, pushing them to both represent the best interests of teachers and the communities in which they teach.

---

2 Ibid., pp 183–93.
3 Ibid., pp. 37–38.

The United Progressive Caucus is a study in the tension *(1)*
between the poles of conservative and confrontational, staff/
leadership-led and teacher-led, self-interested and commu-
nity-centered styles of unionism. It was formed as an
amalgamation of several racial justice caucuses in the early
1970s and held power for nearly four decades. Like much of
the labor movement, the union under the UPC eventually lost
its broad social justice vision but was willing to occasionally
use militant tactics to win gains for members: the caucus led
the union through five strikes over the course of a decade and
a half, including one in 1987 that lasted nineteen days. UPC
leadership negotiated some large economic gains for CTU
members, particularly under Jacqui Vaughn, who became
president in 1984. After Vaughn's death in 1994, Vice President Tom Reece took her place. Vaughn had what her obituary
in the *Chicago Tribune* referred to as "cult-like adoration"
from the union's membership; Reece, however, was seen as
too prone to capitulation to the Board of Education.

Jesse Sharkey, the CTU's current vice president, who was
a high school teacher at the time, saw the UPC leadership
negotiate a contract in 1998, a full ten months before it
expired, "without so much as a single rally. It was pitiful." He
and other reform-minded unionists were drawn to a reform
caucus that would go on to challenge the UPC.

In 2001, the ProActive Chicago Teachers (PACT) *(2)*
caucus unseated the UPC, promising progressive reform.
Debbie Lynch, a white elementary school teacher who
previously directed the CTU's Quest Center for teacher
development, had run as an oppositionist within the union

for years, drawing on the discontent of varied groups of
rank and filers. She ran on a platform of ending corrup-
tion, increasing the union's role in training teachers, and
restoring bargaining rights over noncompensation issues
that had been lost in the 1990s—a kind of liberal reform in
a union that had drifted into conservatism and lost ground
for its members.

PACT's election brought a shift from the conservative
UPC. But Lynch's tenure at the helm of the union would be
brief, and the 2003 contract fight would seal her fate. She
negotiated a contract that, by many accounts, included
decent raises but also entailed increases in health-care costs.
She sold it, however, not as an imperfect recesssion-era
agreement that included some wins and some losses but as a
nearly flawless contract; and she attempted to ram approval
through the union's House of Delegates. She hired an
outside public relations firm to produce several videos to be
shown to the union's membership, trying to market the
contract as a good deal.

"You asked me to bring home the bacon," Lynch said at
the time, in words that almost any CTU activist and staffer
can still repeat today, "and we brought home the whole
hog." Members from both outside and within her own
caucus disagreed, feeling that they had been sold a bill of
goods, and revolted against the proposal, voting overwhelmingly to reject the contract. Lynch, not wanting to
face the press and the Board of Education with the news
that her membership had attempted to overrule her, tried
to ratify the contract despite the house's disapproval. It

was a fiasco; Lynch's autocratic behavior contrasted sharply with the reform mantle she had claimed. Supporters like Sharkey, who favored democratic reform efforts, left the caucus.

The contract was eventually approved, but Lynch's fate as president was largely sealed. In addition to the members' discontent around the contract, she was unable to neutralize the virulently antireform efforts of much of her staff, many of whom were members of the UPC and were engaging in what Norine Gutekanst, a teacher and PACT executive board member at the time, referred to as a "sabotage movement within the union." Just weeks before PACT took over the union, the lame-duck UPC president worked with the union's staff to form another independent union—one that would protect the staff from firings while it tried to sabotage efforts to reform the union.

"We erred on the side of having open arms," Gutekanst, a former bilingual education teacher who is now CTU organizing director, said of the unionized staffers. "And we shouldn't have, because these folks were trying to destroy us."

"And it was those of us who were on the Left who tended to take those positions," said Debbie Pope, another former PACT member and current CTU staffer who had taught for several decades.

Lynch, one of the few constant voices of critique of the UPC, had maintained an opposition caucus for several years. But her vision of reform for the union did not entail a radical shift in how the union operated. "Her critique of the old guard wasn't that it was a service model. She just felt that she could be more competent, hard-working, and honest than them," said Sharkey.

"She was a classic liberal reformer—a technocrat," said Jackson Potter, who became a teacher during the Lynch administration.

> She didn't think she'd have to have a program about union democracy, or engagement of members in entirely different ways, or resistance at the school level, or establishing a culture of solidarity. She thought bringing in ethical people would be enough to engender a cultural change in the union and increase our leverage over the Board of Ed and the corporate forces against us. But that vision wasn't going to stop this tremendous attack on our profession and on schools.

Without shifting the way the union engaged with its members, introducing a new culture of union democracy and member-led governance and action, and preparing for the inevitable counterattack from the union's conservative elements, the limits of PACT's liberal vision were quickly reached and the group was sunk.

In 2004, the year after the contract's negotiation, the UPC returned to power, with Marilyn Stewart assuming the presidency for the next six years. Like Reece, Stewart failed to capture the imagination of the union's members and would oversee the negotiation of another particularly unpopular contract in 2007—one that saw Stewart ask for the yeses at a House of Delegates meeting, then run out of the meeting before the no vote could be called. She then declared to reporters that a contract had been settled and a strike averted, while a crowd of several hundred angry union delegates, including CORE members, chanted "No! No! No!" (with some actually burning physical copies of the contract) outside of Stewart's press conference.[4]

Amid the chaos, a group of activist teachers who had learned from the failures of the Lynch administration were beginning to get organized.

A former history teacher, Jackson Potter is a slender, bearded man who grew up in Chicago yet somehow gained a mysterious accent that much of the city's labor movement finds untraceable. He grew up in a family of radical activists, including a leftist Teamster father and an activist lawyer mother. He began teaching in 2002. Soon, he found himself and his students on the receiving end of neoliberal education reform: His school, Englewood High School on the city's South Side, was facing closure. A union delegate, Potter gave multiple speeches at meetings of the union's House of Delegates to try to drum up support from the union and its members to fight the school's closure. The union, however, continued to do little.

---

4 George N. Schmidt, "Hundreds of Teachers, YouTube Video, Contradict Press Reports on Chicago Teachers Union August 31 Meeting," *Substance News*, September 2007, substancenews.net. Footage of Marilyn Stewart's press conference announcing the approval of the contract and explaining that she made "a parliamentary decision" to not hold an official vote on the contract while a crowd of angry teachers outside can be heard chanting, then seen tearing up and burning the contract: "Chicago Teacher's Union Chaos Part 1 of 2," YouTube.

After one meeting, Potter was approached by Sharkey—another delegate and a teacher at Senn High—whose school was threatened with conversion into a public military academy. The two had seen each other at past union meetings, and Sharkey wanted to discuss the possibility of collaborating. In 2004, CEO Arne Duncan and Mayor Richard M. Daley introduced Renaissance 2010 to Chicago Public Schools; it was a plan first to shut down and later "turn around" low-performing and underutilized schools by firing all the former staff and converting the majority into charter schools run by private operators. Sharkey began traveling around the city to talk to groups of parents, educators, and other activists to publicize the upending effects that Ren2010's closures and turnarounds would have on teachers and neighborhood schools.

After Sharkey and Potter continued agitating among the membership and against the leadership around the union's inaction, the leadership relented, creating a committee to address Ren2010. Both Potter and Sharkey were made members of that committee, along with other teachers at schools targeted for closure. They and a few other like-minded teachers organized education forums on the subject, inviting community members and teachers to attend. They persuaded the union to provide buses and do some basic turnout to give testimony at public hearings and a few small rallies, "but that's as far as it went," said Potter.

Unknown to Potter and Sharkey, the union had formed Chicagoans United for Education (CUE), a community-labor coalition ostensibly to focus on Ren2010 and school closures, and chaired by a union staffer with little power. No one from the union had told either Potter or Sharkey—who were among the members most actively engaged in the very issues the coalition was tasked with addressing—about CUE's existence. Like many conservative union leaders, CTU staff were likely wary of activist members who might attempt to push the union's agenda beyond the boundaries narrowly defined by the official leadership. The more union members like Potter and Sharkey pushed, the worse the elected leaders looked—putting them in danger of losing future elections to upstart activists. After those activists agitated to simply be allowed to attend the coalition's meetings, the union grudgingly let Potter, Sharkey, and another delegate at a closing school, Tony Walden of Bunch Elementary, join the meetings on behalf of the union.

As a result, the three discovered that while the community groups were interested in mounting an effective fight against Ren2010 through rallies, organizing at the neighborhood level, and taking on the district in the press, union leadership was not.

"They were more committed to things like a back-to-school concert with [the rapper] Common," Potter said. Entering into battle with the district over the closures was not a priority; the union seemed to be willing to allow closures and turnarounds to continue unchallenged and did not want CUE to become a body that would begin that kind of battle.

The three immediately began pushing other union representatives in the coalition to take stronger action. Community group representatives said they agreed with the union members—why didn't the union's leadership? Seeing the growing dissatisfaction with their leadership within the coalition and fearing that it could be used to fight them, the union dismantled CUE.

The small group of activists left over from the coalition began building on their relationships with community groups throughout the city. The Kenwood-Oakland Community Organization, headquartered in a gentrifying African American area of the city's South Side, sat in on CUE meetings and had long been active in matters of education. They began working with the small group of activist teachers. Potter sat on the board of the Pilsen Alliance, a community organization in a Mexican immigrant neighborhood, and they too became involved. Blocks Together, a community organization in the Puerto Rican neighborhood of Humboldt Park, Teachers for Social Justice, the policy group Design for Change, and the group Parents United for Responsible Education joined as well. These groups and others had already been organizing community members to show up at hearings about school closures that had been part of Ren2010 and had testified against the closings. The group of dissident teachers and community members pressured the union to act on Ren2010, the school closures, and issues outside of teachers' pay and benefits that were affecting CPS families.

The coalition grew, but its activities were not enough to save Potter's South Side school: one day in 2005 Potter walked into Englewood High and saw the union's Vice President Ted Dallas, who told him the school would be closing and that the union's hands were tied. "This doesn't look too good," Potter recalled Dallas saying. "There's really not much we can do."

At that moment, Potter realized that there were no

prospects for reform within the current union leadership. It would continue to witness the advance of free market education reform, the closing of schools, and the firing of teachers without mounting a fight.

"This is not a fighting union," Potter remembered thinking. "There's not a bone in its body where it's willing to put itself out there on behalf of its membership or on big public policy issues that affect large swaths of public schools across the city."

He and other activists would have to create that fighting union themselves.

The impetus to convince others that this was the case would be provided at a union-sponsored press conference in early 2008 with Dal Lawrence, the former president of the Toledo Federation of Teachers. Amid the fight by activists like the still loosely affiliated coalition of rank-and-file teachers and CPS parents—who were working to keep neighborhood schools open, and to prevent hundreds of educators from losing their jobs—the union presented its idea for reform: fire one tenth of the city's teaching workforce.

"The way to improve schools is to improve teaching," Potter remembered Lawrence saying in his speech, "and the way to do that is to fire 10 percent of the staff." Union President Marilyn Stewart nodded approvingly; she supported the plan.

Potter had grown accustomed to union acquiescence in corporate reform efforts, but this proposal left him dumbstruck.

In early 2008, he and a few other educators called a small group of like-minded activist teachers together at the United Electrical Workers hall, west of the city's downtown, home to the left-wing union whose workers occupied their Republic Windows and Doors factory in protest of layoffs in 2008. Potter and Al Ramirez, another teacher activist, began the night with a tape of the press conference with Lawrence. After the tape ended, Potter addressed the group.

"This is our union's solution to the problems we face," he recalled saying. "Do any of you agree with this solution? All these community partners raising hell all these years, and this is how our union wants to deal with this?"

No one disagreed that the union's response was beyond pitiful, even actively hostile. But some in the gathered group were skeptical about possibilities beyond continued engagement with the union leadership, like forming an opposition caucus to force leadership to the left or vying for power themselves. A few previous members of the Lynch administration were present; a few years earlier they had taken power only to immediately lose it after one term. Others came from socialist political traditions accustomed to "boring from within," engaging with existing leadership and attempting to push them left rather than mounting open opposition to them.

"My position was, that's not possible," Potter said. "These people will destroy our union before we have a chance to make anything happen."

The teachers who had gathered remained skeptical, but

they were intrigued by the prospect of taking the reins of the union. Among the less than a dozen educators present, the idea had been planted.

Since losing his teaching position, Potter had enrolled in a history graduate program where he heard about the annual conference of the Trinational Coalition, a coalition of American, Canadian, and Mexican teachers unions. It was there in 2008 that he first encountered Jinny Sims, president of the British Columbia Teachers Federation. Sims led an illegal strike of 44,000 teachers against a liberal government in British Columbia in 2005; in the face of potential jail time, she and the rest of the union successfully assembled a community coalition to support the teachers and defeat the liberal government's demands.

The parallels were clear: Chicago teachers, like British Columbian teachers, were facing brutal attacks on their profession and on public education by liberal parties—those who were supposed to be their friends. A pushback against those attacks could be carried out in Chicago in ways similar to how Sims's union had: by building genuine, deep ties to communities outside the teaching profession.

A few months later, the group invited Sims to come to Chicago to speak to the group of activist teachers, pooling their money to pay for her plane ticket from Canada. Sims met for five hours with a group of about two dozen CTU activists.

"She spelled out a program for how you really engage with and activate members," Potter said. "She talked about how to take on a moribund political system and a political party that doesn't really represent the interests of workers and poor folks."

Potter recalls a story Sims told about her husband insisting that they transfer the title of their house to his name, just before the illegal strike, to ensure that their property would not be seized by the government. She refused, arguing that she would have to take a principled stance to put herself and her husband in harm's way if they were going to ask the same of their members.

That night they held a forum down the street from the library, at the community center Casa Aztlan, attended by 115 teachers and parents from twenty schools. The forum was put on by a new group who now had given themselves a name: the Caucus of Rank-and-File Educators, or CORE. The loose affiliation of teachers that Potter, Sharkey, and others had started organizing a few years before was now an official organization.

A pamphlet circulated at the time features a crude rendition, hand-drawn by Potter, of an apple gnawed to its core—projecting less an image of scrappy teachers with fire in their bellies than a group worn down to its bones by nonstop attacks from without. The slogan beneath the apple contained an unfortunate typo: "A union that actually fights its members."

Graphic design and copyediting shortfalls aside, CORE pushed forward. They began holding regular meetings. They held multiple forums on cuts to public education. They continued building relationships with community organizations fighting school closures. Membership grew into the dozens. They held a study group on Naomi Klein's *The Shock Doctrine*, which argues that neoliberal reform is pushed by elites during times of political crisis, when the population is disoriented. Potter described the study group as "a light bulb going off": The teachers realized that "education reform" was being carried out in the same way as other attempts to destroy public goods through the free market throughout the world.

CORE's membership, and the political consciousness of those members, was growing, but according to Potter, attempting to take leadership was not yet on the agenda.

"We knew that if there was an opportunity, maybe we would figure out a way to do it, but most of us really didn't have that experience in a big bureaucracy. We were all rank and file who had been activists."

In late 2008, CORE members had obtained, from CPS's central office, a leaked list of the schools slated for closure the next year; they then began organizing teachers in those schools to join the caucus and fight the closings. In January 2009, CORE held a massive public forum on education reform in Chicago. In the middle of a blizzard, some five hundred people, including hundreds of teachers whose schools were soon to be closed, attended.

Surveying the widespread anger of teachers at the union's refusal to fight and CORE's abilities to mobilize teachers and community members, caucus members realized that they actually might stand a chance at taking the leadership on.

CORE, still regularly attending school closure hearings and

giving speeches alongside affected parents, eventually formed the Grassroots Education Movement (GEM). It was a replacement of sorts for CUE, which had been dismantled by the CTU leadership. The caucus functioned as a kind of parallel leadership within the union, taking on the kinds of organizing projects among the union membership and with community members that the union staff was unwilling to support.

CORE had become comfortable with its role as a caucus in open opposition to the UPC's current leadership, and fully embraced the idea of running against the old guard. They held a nominating convention in August 2009, choosing Karen Lewis as their presidential candidate and Potter as their vice president. (Later, because of challenges led by the UPC over his eligibility to run for union office, Potter would step down, to be replaced by Jesse Sharkey.)

But throughout much of that year, the caucus remained unsure about its ability to actually defeat the incumbents in an election. They would have a practice run in a November pension trustee election—a usually boring race where an incumbent had never, in the history of the CTU, been defeated.

On hearing that CORE was to run two candidates in the election, Debbie Lynch told Potter not to waste his time. "Nobody ever wins those. You can do it, but I wouldn't bother," he recalled her saying.

Treating the election with utmost seriousness, CORE mounted a real campaign to elect its two candidates, Jay Rehak and Lois Ashford. They began a get-out-the-vote effort and sent out mailers to all union members reading "Vote J-Lo." Both candidates won.

Shocked, members began looking toward the union's general election in May 2010. "We're thinking we can win this," said Potter.

> The other opposition parties don't think so. They assume their name recognition is enough—that we got lucky in the pension election and we'll soon implode. When it comes down to the serious question of who's going to defend their interests, there's no way [members] are going to pick the inexperienced, radical group.

Still, the leaders of other caucuses recognized CORE's organizing abilities and sought to siphon off some of their key leaders by adding them to the existing caucuses' leadership.

"All of these caucus leaders say, 'We'll go in a backroom and put together a slate'" that includes some CORE candidates, Potter said. "And we say, 'No. We actually are starting to get lots of members. We might actually be able to beat you.'" What's more, factional fights that began within the UPC had come to a head in 2008, with some caucus members expelled from the UPC going on to form their own caucus—likely splitting the UPC vote and presenting a new opportunity for the radical challengers.

On January 9, 2010, CORE hosted another mass-education forum, at Malcolm X College, where the caucus made their official announcement: They would run for union leadership in the May election.

*   *   *

In the spring of 2010, CORE began to make its case to the
CTU membership. It established a campaign to blanket the
city's schools in order for CORE members to reach out to the
rank and file. The UPC had relied on a top-down campaigning model for decades; it entailed simply sending members of
a leadership slate to a small number of the nearly 700 schools
in the CPS. But CORE created a decentralized field campaign
with more than a dozen trained members giving presenta-
tions simultaneously throughout the city. The UPC stood
little chance of winning against such a campaign, lacking the
required trained staff, whereas CORE had many members
who were well able to speak to teachers about the caucus.

Recognizing the insurgent caucus's vastly superior ground
game, the UPC actually turned to CPS officials to try to
prevent CORE and other caucus challengers from organizing, colluding with principals to stop caucuses from
campaigning on school grounds. The union worked hand-in-
glove with the administration to maintain its leadership
positions, leading to confrontations between principals and
CORE activists at schools as well as threats of arrests.

Debbie Lynch, the former CTU president, filed a lawsuit
against these practices so that her own caucus, PACT, could
campaign. Email correspondence was subpoenaed for the
case, which revealed that CTU officials had named CORE
activists like Potter in exchanges with CPS to single them out
for discipline because of their campaigning. Again, Potter
was shocked.

"The fucking union was working with management to
displace members!" he remembered. "There was an

active collaboration between the union and management to take us down!" The conservative leadership was willing to go to surprising lengths to prevent the radicals from winning.

The lawsuit was successful, ending the prohibition of campaigning on school grounds by caucuses. CORE continued making their case to CTU membership, and on CTU's election day, May 22, 2010, CORE took 31 percent of the vote to the UPC's 32 percent, with three other competing caucuses winning the rest. CTU bylaws required an outright majority to win an election, leading to a runoff vote that CORE won handily, taking over 60 percent of the vote. The dissidents had triumphed.

Immediately after she got news of the victory, President-elect Karen Lewis outlined her caucus's vision.

"Corporate America sees K–12 public education as a $380 billion trust that, up until the last ten or fifteen years, they haven't had a sizable piece of," Lewis stated. "Our union . . . didn't point out this simple reality: What drives school reform is a singular focus on profit. Not teaching, not learning—profit." That drive for profit was what the union would directly confront.

"This election shows the unity of 30,000 educators standing strong to put business in its place: out of our schools," Lewis said.[5]

*   *   *

---

5 Ramsin Canon, "Caucus of Rank-and-File Educators (CORE) Takes Over Chicago Teachers Union," *Gapers Block*, June 12, 2010, gapersblock.com.

Upon her election as CTU president, Lewis stated that CORE would "change this into a democratic union responsive to its members." Restructuring began immediately.

Union leadership sought to activate its members and involve them in its own democratic processes in a far more profound and widespread way than had ever been done before; it also initiated a shift in the way the union interacted with its members. In the past, the union had operated under a "servicing" model, where the union's staff handled whatever problems teachers faced in the classroom or with an administrator; if the teacher faced no problems, interaction with union staff was unlikely. Now, teachers themselves were going to be carrying out the union's broad agenda for educational justice.

This was accomplished in part by shifting resources away from representation and toward a new union organizing department, which had never previously existed. And to fund that department and other union projects, staff cut their own salaries and benefits significantly. In years past, union staff's pay and benefits were far greater than union members'; staff pay would now be pegged to classroom teachers' pay.

Leadership broadened the rights and responsibilities of members in the governing House of Delegates. Fourteen member-led committees, from political action to media, were tasked with central roles in the union's day-to-day functioning. A new training program prepared delegates and members for union organizing and governance. The department began a summer organizing internship program that trained several dozen activist teachers to go out to organize their coworkers, many of whom had no prior involvement in their union.

Contract committees made up of activist teachers and delegates were set up at each school, and each committee member was responsible for communicating with 10 other educators face-to-face, including school employees like cafeteria workers, who were members of other unions. Those committees were encouraged to develop their own actions and engage with parents and community members— a kind of organizing that had never been done in the union previously. Members of the House of Delegates, the union's representative body of teachers, received training in bread-and-butter issues like contract enforcement but also, beyond the classroom, in how to fight against school closures. The union also made publicly funded corporate subsidies, most notably through the city's Tax Incremental Financing (TIF) system, a major issue and worked alongside community groups and other unions to expand the CTU's organizing beyond even educational justice to include the issue of inequality and austerity for poor neighborhoods of color throughout the city.[6]

Soon after CORE's victory, the Board of Education demanded that the union either give up a contractually negotiated pay raise or face layoffs while, around the same time, it

6 For an overview of the shifts in the union after CORE took power, see Norine Gutekanst, "How Chicago Teachers Got Organized to Strike," *Labor Notes*, December 2012. For another assessment of CORE, see Rob Bartlett, "Creating a New Model of a Social Union: CORE and the Chicago Teachers Union, *Monthly Review*, June 2013.

was demanding a longer school day, meaning that the board wanted more work for less pay. When the union refused, 1,500 teachers were laid off. The necessity of a strike to beat back the board was becoming clearer, and the union used the layoffs to continue mobilizing members internally.

Charlotte Johnson, a paraprofessional, became an activist in the union when she was recruited by CORE members to the summer internship program, knocking on doors and having conversations in teachers' homes, and organizing community forums for parents about educational inequality in the city. During her two decades as a parapro, no union official had reached out to her to try to involve her in the union. "I can't even remember what the president's name was," she said, referring to the UPC era. As she became more involved, her view of the union shifted: "I want to empower [other members] to do more on their own, not just to wait around for the union to tell them to do something."

Brandon Johnson, a middle school history and reading teacher, knew nothing about the union's internal politics for years. Like many teachers, he was overwhelmed by his responsibilities inside the classroom; although he came from a union family, the CTU was nowhere on his radar.

"When the union doesn't require you to be active outside of your own issues as a teacher, you don't know what to demand of your union," he said.

A colleague who was a CORE member reached out to him in 2010 about that year's election, encouraging him to vote for the caucus and explaining that CORE would push a kind of teachers' unionism that dealt with issues beyond the classroom. Johnson was teaching at a school that seemed a potential target for closure, and the union's potential for fighting the closing soon dawned on him.

"This [CORE] leadership sees itself as a vehicle to stop those closings," he remembered thinking. The UPC did not.

CORE has played a key role in shifting teachers' consciousness about their roles as educators. For years, Brandon Johnson paid little attention to issues beyond his own group of students and his ability to help a few of them gain admission to selective high schools.

"You get isolated in your classroom, and that causes you to focus on individual students," Johnson said. "You begin to judge your accomplishments as a teacher by your ability to help a handful of individual students."

The work of CORE eventually helped him realize that the unionized teachers' work needed to be collective liberation.

"The previous administration maintained that all we can do is help individual students. To challenge a system that does not provide quality schools for all of its students was not on the table." With CORE, "it became a collective struggle rather than an individual struggle."

Since winning control of the union in 2010, CORE has continued its work. Unlike many rank-and-file caucuses that mount successful leadership challenges and then disband after winning—like the briefly successful reform attempts among the Chicago Teamsters in the 2000s—CORE has stayed active, recruited new members, trained new leaders in the internal structures of the union, and discussed and debated the nature of education reform and how to confront it through study groups and book talks. The caucus serves as a space where a radical vision of teacher unionism can be advanced.

"It gives us opportunities to talk more explicitly about the role of people who have left tendencies in the union," Potter said. "Within CORE, we can be unabashedly clear about those politics."

CORE members currently hold power within the union, but members who are now leadership and staffers in the union have stepped down from the caucus's executive board. While union leadership still exerts a strong influence in CORE, formal power has been given to a new layer of leadership.

In many ways, the caucus serves a role similar to the one served by organized left groups during upsurges of radical unionism in the United States, as during the 1930s or 1970s, when leftists played key roles in workplace activism, strikes, and challenges to union leadership. It forms a principled political base that guides the union's work and serves as a check on union officials. The caucus brought an insurgent leadership into power, but has acted independently of it, mounting criticisms when CORE members felt that it was succumbing to the tendency for union leaders to embrace bureaucracy and top-down governance.

"People saw the potential for going down a path of traditional business unionism," Potter said. "CORE has served as a corrective during those moments."

The fight over Senate Bill 7 (explained in full in Chapter 2) serves as an example. In 2011, a bill designed to strip the CTU of much of its power was being pushed in the state legislature by the free market reform group Stand for Children, and the union was to be at the table in Springfield, the Illinois capital. It was the first foray for Lewis, the newly elected president, who a few months earlier had been teaching chemistry and contemplating retirement. In fact, much of the entire leadership of the union would be involved in high-stakes negotiations opposite seasoned machine politicians and shrewd, billionaire-funded education reformers.

As Stand for Children CEO Jonah Edelman explained bluntly during a discussion at the Aspen Ideas Festival in June 2011,[7] the bill was designed to severely limit the CTU's power. It included new rules on teacher layoffs, evaluations, tenure, and other issues that corporate education reformers had long hoped to impose on Chicago's teachers. But most important, by setting the bar for a strike approval far above a simple majority, the bill's sponsors aimed to make a teachers' strike impossible.

"The union cannot strike in Chicago. They will never be able to muster the 75 percent threshold needed to strike," Edelman smugly stated.

The leadership team sent Lewis to the state capitol with

---

7 As Edelman said repeatedly during the speech, he did not expect his comments to ever reach anyone from the CTU or much of anyone beyond the Aspen Festival. His comments were first highlighted by Chicago education blogger Fred Klonsky, whose initial post led to widespread mainstream media coverage and an eventual apology from Edelman. Highlights of the video can be viewed at YouTube: "Stand for Children Co-founder Describes Illinois Take Down of Teachers and Their Unions."

only a union lawyer who had little experience in such negotiations; she went into battle without a large portion of the
union's membership to back her up (largely because the
stakes of the bill and the intentions of its backers like Edelman were not fully understood at the time) or significant
member input into the terms of the bill. Lewis herself later
called the bill's passage "a steamroll job" by reformers,
saying she was bullied by state legislators into accepting
their terms of the law. But not knowing the full details of
the law and its designed intent, Lewis gave the union's official endorsement to Illionis Senate Bill 7 (SB7).

When union members in Chicago heard of the bill's
details, many were incensed. Members recognized that the
bill was devastating—true to its designers' intent, among
other things, it seemed to make a strike effectively impossible. Rather than uncritically backing the leadership they
had just worked for years to elect, CORE members began
an internal discussion between the rank and file and union
leadership. Sarah Chambers, a Chicago elementary
teacher and activist in CORE, remembers the internal
discussion in CORE's steering committee as having been
"heated." After an internal debate that Chambers remembers having lasted for several months, the caucus insisted
that the union would need to reopen negotiations on the
bill. At a House of Delegates meeting, a CORE member
introduced a motion to overturn the union's endorsement
of the bill.

   Chambers says Lewis was not defensive about the move.

"I am not the union—you guys are the union. You're sa
that we need to remove our name from this, so I'm going to
listen to my members," Chambers recalls Lewis saying.
"Other caucuses and other leadership would have never
done that."

Lewis returned to Springfield and reopened negotiations
on SB7, where some of the bill's most draconian provisions
were scaled back, including an actual lowering of the strike
authorization threshold to 75 percent of union members.

Faced with the potential to go down a path of top-down
unionism and uncritical support of leaders, CORE members
balanced backing their leadership while ensuring its fealty to
its left, bottom-up principles.

Successfully capitalizing on members' discontent with
centrist unionism by mounting a leadership challenge from
the left is a monumentally difficult achievement in its own
right. If radicals wrest control of their union, they are faced
with endless problems of running a massive union bureaucracy, for which years in a factory, hospital, or classroom
have not prepared them. The natural impulse for the
supporters of such a group is to close ranks around their
leaders, against whom attacks from the boss and the reactionary elements within the union never stop. CORE has
managed to simultaneously defend and support its leadership in power and to maintain an open environment to
criticize that leadership, to ensure it does not succumb to
the conservative forces facing any union.

The Rank and File

While CORE activists based their caucus on the lessons of failed attempts to reform the CTU and the objective conditions faced by Chicago educators in the early twenty-first century, they were also drawing from a long lineage of labor radicals who had transformed their unions into militant, democratic organizations—not just through leadership challenges to replace conservative leaders with progressives but through the building of rank-and-file worker power independent of the union bureaucracy.

Adherents to this strategy see the stratum of labor leadership, the "bureaucracy" highly prevalent in American unions, as having its own set of interests separate from those of the union members, leading leadership to often act on behalf of their own interests rather than those of the workers so as to reproduce their power and prestige—and, often, their wealth. Thus it is often necessary for labor radicals to fight both the boss, attempting to extract more and more profit from them, and the union bureaucracy, who will attempt to clamp down on any kind of worker activity that could loosen its grip on power and threaten its privileged position as the "working-class aristocracy."

Such organizing has often been carried out by socialists throughout American labor history, from the pitched union battles during the Great Depression up to the twenty-first century. In 1934, facing conservative union leadership at the international and local levels, radical Teamsters in Minneapolis organized workers independently of official leadership to—in the words of socialist leader and rank-and-file organizer Farrell Dobbs—"aim the workers' fire straight at the employers and catch the union bureaucrats in the middle." (Some CTU staffers and activists held a study group on *Teamster Rebellion*, Dobbs's book, in the lead-up to the 2012 strike.) Eventually the strategy led to not only a string of organizing victories headed by rank-and-file workers but also the Minneapolis general strike of 1934—an event that never would have come to pass if the dissidents had simply attempted to gain leadership rather than transform their local from the bottom up.

In 1976, members of the International Brotherhood of Teamsters formed the reform organization Teamsters for a Democratic Union (TDU). Its aim was to capitalize on rank-and-file anger at corrupt and inept union leadership by posing repeated challenges like no votes on dismal contracts and forming independent worker committees on issues facing long-haul truckers and other members of the union. Nearly two decades after its founding, after years of organizing workers independent of the union bureaucracy, the TDU played a key role—in the first democratic election in the union's history—in electing Ron Carey as the Teamsters' international president. This was the election that led to the successful national United Parcel Service strike in 1997 and eventually tipped the balance of power in the AFL-CIO, kicking out Lane Kirkland, its deeply conservative president, in 1995.[8]

---

8 Dan La Botz, "The Tumultuous Teamsters of the 1970s" in *Rebel Rank and File: Labor Militancy and Revolt from Below During the Long 1970s*, Aaron Brenner, Robert Brenner, Cal Winslow, eds., Verso, 2010.

Such rank-and-file efforts today are often associated with the organization Labor Notes and have been carried out by everyone from New York City transit workers in the mid-2000s to New York State nurses today. The key is the recognition of rank-and-file workers themselves as the real movers of reform rather than any individual contender for leadership, no matter how charismatic or politically principled. The CTU is firmly within this tradition of organizing, which helped lead to the overwhelming majority of the union's membership (79 percent in the 2013 union election) backing CORE's confrontational, member-led, leftist style of unionism.

The CTU has grown into a dissident, radical caucus of rank-and-file teachers in strong partnership with community organizations; this is the vehicle that brought its signature brand of confrontational unionism into being. But there were no shortcuts to building the kind of fighting union that the CTU has become in the last three years; many of the caucus's leaders had been fighting this fight for a decade, others far longer. CORE transformed the CTU by educating and agitating teachers about school reform and its place in a broader neoliberal project to dismantle public education, and these now-radicalized rank-and-file teachers would eventually provide the sober vision of what the union was up against—and the kind of confrontational unionism needed to fight it.

At the same time, the union's left leadership positioned the union as a representative of CPS students and their families. Even parents who weren't actively involved in union fights knew of the devastating effects that neoliberal education reform had had on their children, including those due to widespread school closures, particularly in poor neighborhoods of color. When the CTU presented itself publicly as an organization actively and uncompromisingly opposed to such reforms—in an explicit way that had not been done by previous union leadership—and made the case for why they hurt students, CPS parents began to back them. In the public battle over who actually represented the interests of poor and working-class schoolchildren, the union won out over the neoliberal education reformers.

Because education reformers are pushing the consensus on education reform to the right by making their case directly to liberals (the traditional backers of teachers unions), effectively splitting those unions apart from the Democratic Party, teachers unions must appeal directly to the American public, on both local and national levels. This must be done not simply through slick public relations campaigns but through genuine partnership with communities. Teachers unions, guided by a vision of education equality and defending education as a public good, should bargain for improved conditions for all students.

While the blame heaped upon teachers unions for the dismal state of much of the urban education system is certainly disingenuous, used as a justification for a project to dismantle public education, it is also true that teachers unions have largely failed the parents of public school students over the years. Too many teachers unions have pursued agendas of self-interest for decades, focusing solely on bread-and-butter issues even at times of great upheaval among communities outside of schools, from 1960s and 1970s-era conflicts in Newark and the Ocean Hill–Brownsville section of Brooklyn to the CTU itself throughout its history.

Where teachers unions could have played key roles along-side community members fighting for better schools, they often remained neutral or actively hostile to activists' demands, pursuing an agenda that advanced their own interests. The long history of such actions has given the neoliberal reformers a clear opening for attacks.

Teachers unionism without social justice concerns might have been able to survive during the peak of the Keynesian consensus. Now, however, there is a societywide sense that reform requires tacking hard to the right. The only way that collective bargaining in public education can withstand the neoliberal attacks it now faces is to pursue a social movement unionism that genuinely sees its central purposes as fighting for teachers *and* students and preserving public education as a public good.

Otherwise, parents confronted with crumbling schools and unresponsive bureaucracies will continue to see the free-market reformers as the only ones seeming to be seriously concerned about their children's education (disingenuous though they may be); the reformers, meanwhile, will have free rein to continue their attacks on teachers unions, likely with parents' backing.

In short, the only way teachers unions can survive in

the twenty-first century is to adopt the kinds of broad social justice concerns—alongside parents, communities, and others—that the CTU has come to stand and fight for.

2

STRIKE

In the year leading up to September 2012, most Chicagoans familiar with the battles between the Chicago Teachers Union (CTU) and the Board of Education thought a work stoppage would never take place. Neoliberal reformers had worked to pass new laws in the state legislatures attempting to make a strike impossible. Many observers assumed that while the fight between the board and the union would continue at public hearings, in the media, and in the streets, the legal barriers to more militant action were too great.

What's more, common understanding about the use of strikes as a tactic, particularly by public sector workers and *especially* by teachers, suggested that even if a strike were possible, it would be far from prudent. The public, so the narrative went, had turned so far against public workers that a strike could only hurt the latter's chances to win their demands.

Yet on September 9, 2012, Chicagoans turning on their TVs to any local nightly newscast were faced with the very thing the free marketers had tried to make impossible: the sight of CTU President Karen Lewis announcing to the world: "We have failed to reach an agreement that would prevent a labor strike . . . In the morning, no CTU members will be inside our schools. We will walk the picket lines."

As Lewis and the other union leadership left the press conference and walked back through the doors of their downtown offices, a single union member in a red CTU T-shirt stood behind, holding a sign that read "ON STRIKE."

It wasn't supposed to be this way. A strike was supposed to be off the table. And, for most other teachers union locals around the country, it would have stayed there. But over the preceding two years CORE had created an organizing apparatus that blanketed the city's schools, turning a previously unprecedented number of teachers into activists. The newly trained educators then worked to educate and agitate the membership about the gravity of the threats facing teachers and public education broadly, and helped teachers become comfortable with the decision to strike.

The union's leadership was comfortable with industrial action, guided by a left politics and an embrace of confrontational tactics. But given the new legal restraints foisted on the union, intended to make such an action an impossible, a strike would never have come to pass without a previously unprecedented level of development of the union's membership as activists.

Images of Chicago streets overflowing with teachers dressed in red circulated in mainstream media worldwide during and after the strike. But at the time CORE took power, such actions were completely foreign to the union—even under reform leadership.

Jesse Sharkey recalled the union leadership signing a contract in 1998, ten months before its expiration, "without so much as a single rally." A rally to oppose Renaissance 2010 during the UPC administration drew only a few hundred teachers—a tiny percentage of the union's total membership and far from enough to convince any politicians that they were a threat. (Bizarrely, a video from the rally shows the crowd chanting not anti-Ren2010 slogans but the president's name.) If CORE were to take leadership, it would be critical to build an organizational culture in which members felt comfortable with taking control and staging confrontational actions in the streets.

In May 2010, a month before the union's election, CORE organized a mass protest at City Hall. Caucus activists plastered schools with 30,000 fliers, with giant CORE logos on the bottom to make sure that union members knew who was behind the rally. Four thousand showed up, halting traffic in the heart of downtown Chicago at rush hour; there, teachers joyously defied the order of several police officers by leaving the sidewalk and taking to the street. Union officials tried to claim credit for the action, but it was clear that CORE had actually organized it. It was the first time most teachers had engaged in such a mass action. CORE, an independent group, was pushing the kind of action the union leadership itself should have been organizing.

After winning the election, the union needed to make sure that their membership developed a large swath of *ank-and-file leaders. This was done principally through the union's new organizing department, as previously described. Contract committees at each school set up a massive infrastructure enabling members to engage other educators as well as members of other unions working in CPS schools; educators working as summer interns were trained in organizing tactics and fanned out through the city to contact members.

As more members became trained and active in the union, it amped up its actions in the streets: community members took over and eventually shut down a school board meeting with a "mic check" action borrowed from the Occupy movement, where one person yells out a phrase at a time and the gathered group then yells it back; the union joined a coalition of labor and community organizations to march on a Cadillac dealership in a posh neighborhood that had received $7 million in public money through TIF funds, leading to two arrests; parents occupied a school on the city's Northwest Side to protest its designation as a "turnaround;" community groups led a silent march of hundreds on the mayor's home.

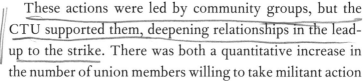

These actions were led by community groups, but the CTU supported them, deepening relationships in the lead-up to the strike. There was both a quantitative increase in the number of union members willing to take militant action and a qualitative shift in CTU members' consciousness beyond individual antagonistic politicians and disinvestment in schools. Members were beginning to connect the dots between city-level policies benefitting corporate elites, the crumbling and economically devastated schools in which they worked, and the broader neoliberal push in Chicago and beyond. They became increasingly willing to push the envelope and take action against the forces behind these policies.

Community organizations were the first to fight against school closures in the city, with rank-and-file teachers later joining on. Similarly, those organizations took a lead in pushing the union toward forming stronger community-teacher coalitions and staging more militant actions.

The Kenwood-Oakland Community Organization, which had been fighting closures for years, was in the vanguard of the march on Mayor Emanuel's house. It was the kind of risky, confrontational action—a descent en masse, with hundreds of community and union members on the mayor's residential block taking their demands to his front door— which, according to some union staffers, the union would probably never have done on its own, for fear of alienating the public, had it not been pushed by an outside group. (A sign of the shifting political winds was an article in the *Chicago Tribune*—a normally reliable outlet for conservatism—where a columnist wrote that she had initially seen the march on the mayor's house as unacceptable but had changed her mind: "the protesters are rightfully frustrated . . . They're within bounds to do what they can, peacefully, to take their views directly to him."[9])

9 Mary Schmich, "Mayor's Home Turf Is Fair Game for Protesters," *Chicago Tribune*, February 22, 2012.

Similarly, parents with Blocks Together, a community organization in the largely Puerto Rican neighborhood of Humboldt Park, occupied Piccolo Elementary School after the board announced that it would become a "turnaround" school. This occupation, supported and attended by the CTU, was successful in that it led to a meeting with the Board of Education. Organizers from Action Now, the former ACORN group in Chicago, encouraged the union to be more ambitious in its organizing and use the cachet it held within communities to expand the scope of its organizing, suggesting a joint organizing campaign with the union against foreclosures in areas near public schools.

The Grassroots Collaborative, an alliance of eleven community groups and unions, insisted that the union tie the crumbling conditions of CPS schools to the TIF program, a public financing method supposedly intended to alleviate blight in poor neighborhoods.[10] Criticizing TIF and its centrality to defunding public education later became central to the union's organizing: Teachers were educated about TIF during the union's summer organizing program, where teachers worked as organizing interns and knocked on the doors of union and community members, engaging in thousands of conversations about the role of corporate tax breaks in defunding education.

---

10   In practice, Tax Incremental Financing (TIF) has robbed public institutions like schools of hundreds of millions of dollars in public funding by giving those funds away to wealthy corporations. TIF is one of the key economic development programs in the city; it has been widely criticized as a slush fund for the current and former mayors of Chicago, who have doled out much of the funds (at least $1.7 billion in 2013) to wealthy corporations. See Ben Joravsky and Mick Dumke, "The Shadow Budget," *Chicago Reader*, October 22, 2009.

The union's education reform proposals included strong critiques of TIF; billionaire Hyatt Hotel heiress and school board member Penny Pritzker was targeted after a South Side Hyatt received over $5 million in TIF funds. The CTU's focus on TIF, at the Collaborative's encouragement, ended up activating a number of members and became the focus of multiple public actions—including the previously mentioned action at a Cadillac dealership (a TIF recipient) where a union staffer and community member were arrested—and one mass march during the strike. Focusing on TIF helped make the issue of massive public subsidies to wealthy corporations at the expense of schools and other public institutions a much-discussed public issue in Chicago.

Community organizations pushed the CTU to broaden its focus to issues that affected the entire working class and to take more militant action—two aspects of their organizing that were central to their ability to win the strike, gain the trust of average Chicagoans, and build power as a union.

While the union built its membership capacity, however, free market reformers were working to eliminate the union's ability to strike through SB7.

In June 2011, Jonah Edelman, CEO of Stand for Children (SfC), gave an afternoon talk at the Aspen Ideas Festival,[11] an annual gathering of "thought leaders"

---

11 The talk can be found on YouTube. Edelman clearly did not think his talk would go far beyond the conference participants in the room, laughingly saying that he did not think his comments would get back to CTU President Karen Lewis. The video was initially picked up by Chicago education blogger and former Chicago-area teachers union president Fred Klonsky.

specializing in empty sloganeering masquerading as the cutting edge of critical intelligence. (One quote, featured on the website's home page, reads "If you're stuck, innovate yourself out.")

During the talk, Edelman, whose organization initially came to Illinois at the invitation of billionaire former private equity manager Bruce Rauner, spoke with astonishing candor; he explained calmly the backroom politicking necessary to "jam the proposal down [teachers and their unions'] throats." Soon after its beginnings in Illinois, his organization donated $600,000 to nine state legislative races in an attempt to curry favor with State House Speaker Michael Madigan and to show Madigan that his organization "could be a new partner to take the place of the Illinois Federation of Teachers" after the speaker had passed a pension bill highly unfavorable to teachers in 2010.

Edelman explains that SfC had attempted to gut collective bargaining rights for teachers entirely in a previous lame-duck session; therefore, when he approached teachers union leaders like Karen Lewis—whom he describes as a "die-hard militant"—with new restrictions on teachers union rights that appeared less drastic, he seemed conciliatory. Although Lewis signed onto the bill, she soon faced a revolt from members in her own caucus, who overturned her endorsement and forced her to return to Springfield to renegotiate parts of the law, as previously described, and Senate Bill 7 eventually passed.

Two of the legislation's principal accomplishments were

to significantly limit the issues over which Chicago teachers could legally strike (wages, benefits, and some aspects of evaluation) and to require a seemingly unachievable vote margin to permit a strike. Instead of a simple majority of member *votes* being required to authorize a strike, a 75 percent majority of *all members* was now necessary—a percentage chosen, as Edelman explains in the video, after the SfC examined percentage breakdowns of past strike votes and which it deemed unachievable.

"In effect, they wouldn't have the ability to strike," Edelman says matter-of-factly in the tape. "They will never be able to muster the 75 percent threshold." Outlawing a teachers strike outright was not yet politically feasible; maintaining a chimera of that right while making it all but impossible to achieve was the next best thing.

Edelman knew that teachers would not be able to win the public's support if they were seen as striking over compensation issues. Particularly at a time when the national discourse had turned so sharply against teachers, the CTU would not be able to publicly frame its strike as anything but a public temper tantrum of overpaid workers whose greed had driven them out of their classrooms and onto picket lines.

SfC wanted to deprive the CTU of its right to strike because they knew that the union's ability to withhold its labor was its most powerful tool. With the union, the only body with enough institutional resources to fight back, effectively defanged, SfC could continue apace with their efforts to transform public education.

Jonah Edelman came to the conclusion that the CTU would never be able to achieve a strike because he had parsed the data from the tallies of strike votes in years gone by and— because of the large number of teachers who abstained from voting—had seen that the union had never mustered even a majority of all voting members; three quarters, then, seemed well beyond the realm of the possible. But a slate had never entered the union's leadership with a plan to engage and educate the union's membership the way that CORE did.

Much of the membership had become warmed up in the streets, but, given the new constraints imposed by SB7, the union would have to expand its organizing program if it was going to be able to achieve a strike vote. With a new 75 percent threshold to reach, the union decided it could not go into such a vote without a practice run—both to test its logistical capacity to pull off a strike vote and to indicate to members that a strike could be coming.

The union held that practice vote in January 2012, asking four questions about the board's proposals for teachers' contracts. It garnered 80 percent participation from members, with 98 percent rejecting the proposals.[12] The organizing the union had done since 2010 had paid off.

The practice vote indicated that there was significant momentum within the union for a strike, and they sought to capitalize on it. On May 23, the union leadership called for a huge rally inside one of the city's largest auditoriums, the

---

12   Norine Gutekanst, "How Chicago Teachers Got Organized to Strike," *Labor Notes*, December 2012.

downtown Auditorium Theatre. Four thousand union members packed inside, with another 1,500 rallying on the street outside. An iconic picture of the event shows Karen Lewis from behind at the podium, addressing a mass of teachers in front of her, all in red. As Lewis spoke, a chant of "Strike! Strike! Strike!" went up.

Teachers left the auditorium to join a mass march with other unions and community organizations. The crowd of several thousand slowly moved south on LaSalle Street, approaching the heart of the city's financial district, where Occupy Chicago had set up shop several months earlier. A small group of young Occupy activists jumped in place, chanting, "Go, go, go teachers!" as waves of educators marched by. The teachers appeared ecstatic, both to be taking the streets en masse and to have the support of onlookers.

Just a few years earlier, the union had been unable to mount any kind of effective pushback against a neoliberal education agenda. Now, with thousands of teachers marching through downtown Chicago at rush hour, days after a practice vote revealing a strong willingness to walk off the job, the CTU looked like a union that could pull off a successful strike.

On June 6, the union held its strike authorization vote. Union staff and activists tracked down teachers and staff wherever they were during the summer vacation and, over the course of several days, 92 percent of the membership participated in the vote. The results, announced June 11, were stunning: 90 percent of the entire membership voted to authorize a strike; among those teachers who voted, 98 percent voted in favor of strike authorization.

Teachers went far beyond the vote total deemed impossible by Jonah Edelman and the state legislators who, a year earlier, thought they had prevented a teachers strike from ever happening in Chicago. A strike had now been authorized, allowing for the union leadership to call a strike when it saw fit.

By the time of the strike authorization vote, the board and the union had been in negotiations over the contract for the better part of a year and seemed to be going nowhere. The board wanted to implement a longer school day without a pay raise (on top of a contractually negotiated 4 percent raise that had been summarily taken from teachers the year before), scrap the "steps and lanes" section of the contract (by which teachers received raises for additional education and years worked), and increase teachers' health-care costs, among other concessions. The union rejected these proposals and demanded increased protections for teachers displaced by school closures and better working conditions, like smaller class sizes. In July, a neutral fact finder, brought in to attempt to mediate the negotiations and make suggestions as required by state law, issued a report on the state of contract talks; it was rejected by both the union and the board.[13] With the fact finder's report rejected and a strike authorized, the union leadership could call a strike when it wanted.

---

13 Lorraine Forte, "For the Record: Details on the Fact-Finder's Report," *Catalyst Chicago*, July 19, 2012, catalyst-chicago.org.

Negotiations continued, and the board continued to offer unsatisfactory contract proposals. On August 29, the union issued a ten-day notice, saying that if no satisfactory deals were reached with the board, teachers would strike. No deals were reached.

So on the night of September 9, Karen Lewis and a crowd of solemn-faced teachers gathered outside the union's downtown headquarters to announce to the world that the next day, the union would be on strike, for the first time since 1987.

"We demand a fair contract now," she said. "Until there's one in place, one that our members will accept, we will be on the line."

The CTU called for pickets at local schools to begin at 6:30 a.m. on September 10. Lacking the discipline instilled by more demanding professions (like say, teaching), I couldn't drag myself out of bed at that time. By the time I was on my bicycle heading downtown from the far North Side on Ashland Avenue, a main thoroughfare, picket lines were well under way.

The six-mile ride from my apartment to the Board of Education included scene after scene of teachers chanting and marching outside their schools. The city was blanketed with striking educators, all clad in red union T-shirts. I passed one school with forty or fifty teachers picketing in front, rode a few more blocks, then passed another.

I stopped at the second picket line I saw, at Lakeview High School, with several dozen teachers a few blocks from the mayor's home, to take in the scene. A slim, middle-aged African American teacher in charge of the bullhorn started chanting, "We're going to Rahm's house!" He stopped after chanting it a few times, giggling. But an early-forties white woman, who looked stunningly similar to my ninth grade American history teacher, wasn't laughing.

"No, seriously. It's right over there," she yelled out, pointing west toward Emanuel's residence on Hermitage Avenue. "We should go." Later in the week, those teachers and others in the vicinity would march over to the mayor's house and picket and chant outside of it.

The entire city felt transformed. Teachers were engaged in highly visible, militant mass action, and there was a widespread sense throughout the city of the legitimacy and necessity of such actions—for educators and for other workers.

Rather than having teachers picket at their schools for a few hours in the morning and then head home, as had occurred in previous strikes, the union held mass rallies downtown nearly every day with tens of thousands of teachers and their supporters. After one such march on the strike's first day, I walked into a chain coffee shop and grabbed a yogurt cup. The young cashier sized me up, taking stock of my red T-shirt.

"Are you a teacher?" she asked me.

I looked down at my shirt, stuttering for a moment.

"Oh, uh, I'm actually . . ."

"Go ahead," she interrupted, waving me through the line while other customers behind me watched. "You all are amazing. We support the teachers 100 percent."

The moment of solidarity between a nonunion cashier making minimum wage and a perceived unionized public school teacher on strike seemed too beautiful for me to interrupt with the reality—that I was not, in fact, a teacher, but rather a leftist who enjoyed the teachers' marches—so I started to thank her profusely. The two other cashiers stopped their transactions to turn to me and tell me that they too hoped to see the teachers win.

"I'd be out there, too, if I could," the twenty-something woman told me.

Leaving the café in a rising class-consciousness–induced daze, I put my bike on a bus back to the far North Side and hopped on behind a few other passengers. When my turn to swipe my card came, the driver waved me on.

"Go ahead, sir," he said nonchalantly.

Oblivious, I gestured toward the card reader.

"Oh—is it broken?"

He shook his head. Like the cashier minutes earlier, he gestured to my shirt before waving me to move along without paying.

"We gotta support the teachers."

Such support felt almost universal. I visited nearly two dozen picket lines during the strike and was astounded at the number of supportive honks filling the air at all of them. Friends told stories of walking around the city in red T-shirts and pedestrians stopping them, telling them that the teachers' cause was just. The strike was all the city could talk about.

Where was the atmosphere of hatred for teachers that the free marketers had worked so hard to encourage over the last half-decade or so? Where were the enraged Chicagoans contemptuous of the cushy jobs bankrolled by the hard-earned money sucked out of their checks every other week, publicly confronting teachers on the picket line, or at least flipping them the bird from their cars as they drove by? They were nowhere to be found.

There was a generalized sense throughout the city, whether on picket lines or public transit or on the street, that this group of workers was right to go on strike; that struggle and militant action were justified and to be supported.

The city felt like it belonged to the teachers.

The effects of cadre development within the union soon became clear during the strike: Teachers began organizing actions themselves, largely independent of the CTU leadership.

Kim Walls, a science teacher who had never been active in the union before becoming involved in CORE, attended the union's summer organizing program. It was there that she first heard about TIF and the program's effects on public schools. She was appalled at what appeared to be deliberate starvation of the city's public schools of resources in favor of redistributing wealth upward to some of the city's richest corporations.

On September 14, the union and the Grassroots Collaborative coalition planned a rally against TIF downtown, focusing on billionaire hotel heiress Penny Pritzker, appointed by President Obama to Secretary of Commerce in 2013 and a former appointed member of the Board of Education. Her company,

Hyatt Hotels, had received $5.2 million in TIF funds to build a new hotel in Hyde Park, where Walls lives.

Walls received a call from union staffer Matthew Luskin days prior to the action. "I said, 'Matthew, I'm not going downtown. There's a Hyatt right here.'" She told Luskin she would organize her own protest against Hyatt in Hyde Park. "He just said, 'Go for it.'"

Walls called Hyde Park–area teachers and told them to "call their people" to come out to the action. When the day came, 300 teachers and supporters marched on the hotel— with little to no support needed from union staff.

Teachers throughout the city organized similar actions without the aid of union staffers. No union staffers planned the small marches on the mayor's house during the strike; teachers planned those themselves. After thirty-three of the fifty city council members (all but one of whom were Democrats) signed a letter to Karen Lewis at the strike's beginning, begging the union not to strike, rank-and-file teachers, livid at their aldermen for publicly chastising them and siding with the mayor, independently organized protests in their neighborhoods against them. All were Democrats and several self-identified as progressives, but the teachers didn't care—they had been insulted and were unafraid to organize their own actions to call out those aldermen publicly through street actions.[14]

---

14   Later, several such aldermen—clearly jarred by the swift organizing against them—would change their tune, signing onto letters demanding a moratorium on school closures and supporting other union-backed proposals. The teachers' willingness to confront the Democratic city council members directly paid off.

Mayor Emanuel, the Board of Education, and corporate reform groups like Stand for Children and Democrats for Education Reform (DFER) had worked to try to turn Chicagoans against the teachers union long before the strike began. DFER funded a number of radio ads in the months before the strike, targeting African American and Latino neighborhoods in particular, attempting to preemptively turn parents against the strike. And nationally, of course, the mainstream media had been pushing against teachers unions for years.

But during the strike, polls showed that the public—and parents of color in particular—supported the teachers union by overwhelming numbers. The first poll released showed that among registered voters in Chicago, 47 percent supported the strike while 39 percent did not. By the fourth day, another poll showed similar numbers but noted that 63 percent of African Americans and 65 percent of Latinos—in a city where 91 percent of the public school district is made up of children of color—supported the strike.[15]

The numbers were proof that teachers could win the public to their side and against free market reform despite the hostile climate locally and nationally. Reform groups funded by billionaires could not convince Chicagoans that the teachers were acting against CPS students' interests

15　Kara Spak and Fran Spielman, "47% of Chicago Voters Back Teachers," *Chicago Sun-Times*, September 11, 2012. Second poll data from independent polling organization We Ask America, "As Chicago Teachers Strike Enters Fourth Day, a New Poll Proves Majority of Parents and Taxpayers Approve of Fair Contract Fight," *Chicago Teachers Union*, September 13, 2012, ctunet.com.

because the CTU had made their case directly to those working-class and poor communities of color through its genuine partnerships with groups based in them, and by engaging with and organizing in those communities for years before the strike.

The consensus in Chicago and around the country seemed to be that teachers unions' very existence was hated by most; going on strike was not even an option, since doing so would only serve to further widen the gap between the public and the unions. But the CTU had managed to convince the public that the strike was not reflective of selfishness—it was the very means by which the union would accomplish a progressive education agenda. Neoliberal forces had long attempted to turn average people against public sector unions' struggles by framing any public workers' demands as coming at individual taxpayer's expense; in Chicago, that attempt failed.

After the strike's first week, many Chicagoans assumed that teachers would return to class on Monday. Emanuel had clearly lost the public relations battle. Polls showed strong majorities, especially among CPS parents and Chicagoans of color, backing the teachers by large margins. The union had the upper hand in bargaining, and through the tentative agreement CTU leaders brought to the House of Delegates meeting that Sunday was rumored to contain a number of harmful provisions for teachers, given the broader assault on teachers unions and the austerity generally, it seemed as strong as possible.

But on Sunday, September 16, the House of Delegates did not vote to end the strike. They extended it by two more days.

The union had wrung significant concessions out of a Board of Education that seemed bent on levying a number of significant blows against them. But delegates said their membership had not had enough time to fully examine the proposed deal. The agreement would not be "shoved down our throats," as delegate and first-grade teacher Yolanda Thompson put it.

After the first week, at the Sunday-night House of Delegates vote over whether or not to extend the walkout for two more days, Lewis made no attempt to sell the idea of ending the strike based on the contract's strength. Some of the union's staff were worried that the union would squander the goodwill it had built up among CPS parents, but the leadership did not try to dissuade the membership from extending the strike.

So instead of forcing the membership to decide on a contract they had not read and did not fully understand, delegates extended the strike for the sole purpose of allowing rank-and-file members the full opportunity to comprehend the contract that had been negotiated in their name.

The vote was a victory for union democracy. But union democracy does not always make for good PR: favorable coverage in the mainstream press evaporated. The city's major newspapers and nightly newscasts ran top stories about parents' patience running thin with the union. But on Monday morning, teachers arrived at picket lines outside their schools at 6:30 a.m., eager to review the proposal but lacking a formal process to do so.

Becca Barnes, a ninth-grade history teacher on the South Side, said teachers at her school made photocopies of the contract, stood against a fence, and spent an hour reading through it line by line, circling key sections and commenting in the margins—as though they were grading papers. As they began picketing, the contract was still on their minds. So Barnes and her fellow teachers—about a hundred of them—decided to walk to a nearby park and read it together.

"None of us planned in advance to comb through it collectively," Barnes says. "We were going to just go over highlights," Barnes remembers, "but then someone said, 'No—we need to read the entire contract.'"

So, sitting together at a park, they read through every line, debating the victories and concessions hashed out at the bargaining table.

"It was very emotional," says Barnes. "Some people were sick of striking. Others said, 'This isn't good enough. This one line is reason enough for me to stay out.'"

Similar scenes took place throughout Chicago. For the first time, teachers were studying every word of their contract, the principal document governing their work lives.

"We were genuinely interested in what each other had to say—even the people who wanted to go back," Barnes says. The union voted to ratify the contract October 3, with 79 percent of membership in favor.

The union's decision to extend the strike by two days can be traced in part to practical concerns by the leadership. The membership has a history of punishing leaders who tried to force contracts upon them. For example, there was the time in 2003 when former president and reformer Debbie Lynch lost her reelection bid, having told members that her contract had not just brought home "the bacon" but "the whole hog." And again, there was the angry impromptu rally in 2007, in which some CORE members participated, where members burned copies of the proposed contract. These memories undoubtedly weighed heavily on Karen Lewis and other leaders' minds.

But there was also a clear concern for democratic process that is incredibly rare among American unions—particularly in a situation like contract negotiations, which are almost always seen as battles between union leaders and management negotiators in which the general membership has little part. The strike's extension showed that rank-and-file teachers were firmly in control of the union.

3
THE FUTURE

On the chilly afternoon of September 18, 2012, the parking lot of the union hall housing the CTU's House of Delegates meeting, usually forlorn, was packed with teachers' cars and local and national news trucks. A few days earlier, teachers had voted to extend their strike for two days, so all union members would have the chance to fully digest and debate the proposed tentative agreement between the Board of Education and the CTU; a second vote would now be held to determine whether to call off the strike.

When I arrived, journalists had been milling about for several hours. Local television reporters spoke into their BlackBerrys, informing their editors of nothing; a newsman in a trench coat, perhaps out of boredom, tried holding his ear up against one of meeting room's exit doors multiple times, futilely hoping to catch any words uttered inside. A normally mild-mannered union staffer seemed to be so incensed at this that I worried the strike might see its first casualty in the form of a well-tailored journalist. I somehow allowed myself to be sucked into an argument with an out-of-town pamphleteer accusing the union's leadership of selling out its membership and not holding out on the picket line for the immediate establishment of the dictatorship of the proletariat, or something like that.

Without warning, the doors flew open and a sea of educators in red half walked, half ran through the gauntlet of news cameras and pouncing journalists, some looking terrified as members of the media chased after them rabidly for a quote. In what would become a front-page picture in the *Chicago Tribune* the next day, one teacher in a bright-red sweater emerged through the glass doors clutching copies of the contract in one hand and a raised fist in the other, a look of pure elation on her face. Off to the side, I struck up conversations with several delegates who weren't fleeing; they told me that the members had voted overwhelmingly to go back to work the next day.

I expected these members to share details about the tentative contract's specifics: what they had gained, what they had no choice but to give up on, joys and disappointments about the collective bargaining process. But all of the teachers I spoke with had little interest in discussing the details of bargaining. They wanted to talk about how the union could capitalize on its energized, tightly organized membership to continue leading a fight for broader educational reforms. One teacher, Eric Skalinder, said he wanted to "focus [the union's] energy on fighting privatization, advocating for neighborhood schools, all of it"; clinician Kristine Shanley said that the union now needed to prepare a campaign against charter school expansion through closures, so that "every time [CPS] announces a school closing to turn it into a charter, we're ready to mobilize and fight back."

Teachers had just won a historic strike. Yet few educators seemed interested in celebrating their accomplishments—they were looking more at how to best position themselves in future fights for public education.

On that day, 79 percent of the educators voted to return to work the following morning. Significant noncompensatory provisions that were mutually beneficial to CPS students and teachers were negotiated. Students were now guaranteed textbooks on the first day of class; teachers' supplies budgets were more than doubled; and the proportion of a teacher's evaluation made up by students' standardized testing scores was held to the state's legal minimum despite the board's attempt to increase it. Mayor Emanuel had hoped to introduce merit pay into the contract, but he was denied.

The union also beat back an attempt to increase healthcare costs by 40 percent. The union and Emanuel had battled over a longer school day for months and did agree to extend it, but not without annual raises along with a cost-of-living increase, which the mayor had initially fought.

However, the contract was still far from perfect. Karen Lewis admitted as much. "These are austerity times," she stated on the day of the second vote. "This is an austerity contract."[1]

---

1 "CTU's Karen Lewis: People Don't Always Get Everything They Want in a Contract," WBEZ, September 18, 2012, wbez.org.

The contract contains some key provisions that have since proven damaging to the union. Much of the negotiation occurred over how much CPS would pay out in benefits to teachers who were displaced from a school that was closed. Neither side had any illusions about what lay at the heart of that debate: how expensive it would be for the district to close schools. The more benefits CPS had to pay displaced teachers, the more difficult it would be for them to close large numbers of schools.

"We lost a significant portion of those benefits," said CTU organizer Matt Luskin. "We didn't lose anything near what they wanted, but it became much cheaper to close a school."

Class sizes had been a central issue in the union's education reform proposals and public messaging during the strike. CPS had attempted to remove class size ceilings, set at twenty-eight for kindergarten and thirty-one for upper level grades; the union stopped the district from increasing such levels but could not win any contract provisions to lower the ceilings.[2]

The contract the union ended up negotiating contained both important wins that were mutually beneficial to teachers and students and some deeply flawed provisions with which the Board of Education and the mayor will continue to try to dismantle public education.[3]

---

2 Assumably, the CTU would have made class sizes and other non-monetary concerns an issue during bargaining, but education reform legislation, including SB7 and the Chicago School Reform Amendatory Act of 1995, made such issues "non-mandatory" bargaining issues—CPS was not legally compelled to negotiate over them. See Yana Kunichoff, "Effects of SB7 Collective Bargaining Provisions Being Felt in CTU vs. CPS Negotiations," *Chicago Reporter*, July 19, 2012.

3 For an extensive critical discussion on the final negotiated contract

Such losses are common for unions in the twenty-first century. But the momentum the union carried after the strike's end, into its fights around issues like school closures, was nearly unparalleled in recent labor history. The CTU transformed itself from an organization representing the narrow economic self-interest of teachers into the principal body fighting for educational justice for CPS students—both in the eyes of the public, which came to trust the union's education reform agenda over the mayor's, and in the eyes of its own members, like the ones I spoke with as they left the House of Delegates meeting.

The achievements of the 2012 strike are greater than the contract the union was able to negotiate, and its success is not owed to one tactic. The union was successful because its aims were broad and encompassed the aims of Chicago's entire working class, even while its demands were specific. The CTU took a confrontational stance against the forces pushing for free market–based education reform. Rather than trying to meet such reformers in the middle on their proposals to privatize schools or increase teacher evaluations based on standardized testing—as national teachers unions have done—the CTU was uncompromising in its rejection of the demands of Mayor Rahm Emanuel and corporate reform groups. And rather than allowing such groups to paint the union as a roadblock to educational progress, the CTU put forth its own positive proposals to reform schools, grounded

and other aspects of the strike, see David Kaplan, "The Chicago Teachers' Strike and Beyond: Strategic Considerations" *Monthly Review*, June 2013.

in an unapologetic vision of progressive education that would be funded by taxing the rich. Road maps to victory exist only in hindsight, but the CTU's program can provide some useful guides to teachers unions around the country.

Targeting Neoliberal Education Reform

The push to transform education into a commodity that can be bought and sold on the free market has mirrored the broader neoliberal turn since the 1980s, which has sought to privatize public goods and sell them off to the highest bidder, destroy unions to eliminate workers' opposition to this agenda, and eliminate restrictions to the flow of capital.[4]

In education, neoliberalism has meant a push for the replacement of neighborhood schools with charter schools, expansion of "school choice," merit pay for teachers, a general demonization of educators and efforts to disempower their unions, and an obsession with standardized testing. Corporate management strategies have come to replace concern for pedagogy; teachers are mandated to be principally concerned with measurable results and value-added assessments through test scores,

---

4   A central critique of prominent liberal defenders of public education—like education historian and former US Assistant Secretary of Education Diane Ravitch—is that they do not identify current efforts to introduce free market reforms in education as part of this broader neoliberal project; public school reformers like former Washington, DC, Chancellor Michelle Rhee or foundations like Gates are portrayed as simply uninformed or misguided rather than actively working to undermine education as a collective good. See Lois Weiner, *The Future of Our School: Teachers Unions and Social Justice*, Haymarket Books, 2012; Lois Weiner and Mary Compton, eds., *The Global Assault on Teaching, Teachers, and Their Unions*, Palgrave Macmillan, 2008.

and principals and entire school districts are judged based on their ability to raise test scores.

Teaching itself has become increasingly contingent work, a profession that chews up young educators and spits them out after a handful of years. Teachers are expected to take on additional administrative tasks, while at the same time their class sizes are growing and their planning periods are being whittled away. Teachers' morale is at an all-time low, and teachers are leaving the profession in droves: A 2012 University of Pennsylvania study found that the largest group of teachers in public education had one year of experience.[5] The goal is to make life so unbearable for teachers that they are pushed out of the profession long before they come to expect middle-income salaries or provisions like tenure. Educating students can then be done on the cheap; the teacher with two decades of experience and a master's degree can be replaced with a Teach for America volunteer putting in two years in a poverty-stricken elementary school in order to include it on his or her law school application.

Private foundations with massive resources have taken the lead in pushing this agenda under the guise of a concern for the well-being of America's schoolchildren. Three in particular—the Bill and Melinda Gates Foundation, the Eli and Edythe Broad Foundation, and the Walton Family Foundation—play a central role in shaping education reform policy. Unsurprisingly, these foundations, built on the largesse of three of the country's wealthiest capitalists and their families,

---

5 Will Johnson, "Lean Production," *Jacobin*, Winter 2013.

are pushing hard for free market reforms in public schools. That these foundations could accomplish this through strategic investments of a few billion dollars every year over the last decade or so in a sector whose cost comes to more than half a trillion dollars every year, with almost no accountability to the broader public, is fairly surprising—a testament to how desperately cash-strapped school districts around the country truly are.[6] Waving donations that are equivalent to a tiny percentage of most school districts' annual budgets in front of superintendents staring down massive budget shortfalls seems to be all that is needed to convince administrators to adopt the free market agenda being peddled by these ultrawealthy philanthropists.

Besides making strategic donations directly to schools, these foundations have helped fund organizations that attempt to style themselves as leaders of a movement advocating for poor children of color in crumbling schools, positioning themselves as the children's only advocates against cruel organized groups of grownups trying to rob them of an education. Their websites trumpet slogans like "Renewing Schools, Renewing Neighborhoods," as that of Stand for Children (SfC) does; Democrats for Education Reform (DFER) say, in their statement of principles, that schools "have become captive to powerful, entrenched interests that too often put the demands of adults before the educational needs of children." SfC and DFER, then, are the saviors for these students.

---

6   Joanne Barkan, "Got Dough? How Billionaires Rule Our Schools," *Dissent*, Winter 2011.

These organizations have effectively framed the issue as a battle between two groups: organizations like SfC, DFER, charter school advocates, and others who are pushing for reforms in the best interests of children on the one hand and, on the other, teachers unions, which are consistently throwing up roadblocks to students' well-being in order to defend their own interests.

The goal of these foundations and the policies they have shepherded into the mainstream consensus is to bring education, as a sector, into line with the goals of capital accumulation. The humanistic goals of education—of creating informed citizens capable of creative and critical thinking—have been erased.

Pushback against these policies must include a willingness to confront not only the Republican Party but also the Democrats. The movement to transform public education is often seen as a phenomenon pushed by the right. But the right-wing agenda for education reform—the emphasis on privatizing and deregulating schools, crushing teachers unions and stripping educators of collective bargaining rights, "value added" assessments of teaching, and a general embrace of free market reforms as a panacea for all that ails students—is also, in large part, the Democratic Party's agenda for education reform.

The Democrats have seen the rise of a strong neoliberal wing over the last several decades, and an increasing number of Democrats no longer even pretend to placate unions— once seen as a central constituency for the party—or to concern themselves with a broader agenda of equality and social justice. The party's policies look more and more like those of the Republicans. This is particularly true in the case of education reform, where Democrats have swallowed the right's free market orthodoxy whole. Much of the party appears to have given up on education as a public project.

Education policy's hard tack to the right under Ronald Reagan was continued by his former vice president, George H. W. Bush; Bill Clinton and the New Democrats behind him were happy to follow suit. Today, the Obama administration's policy proposals embrace the kinds of free market reforms and philosophies that were first introduced by the right. Central to Race to the Top, the president's signature education reform program, are cash incentives for states that allow students' performance on standardized tests to be tied to teacher evaluations, and a push for merit pay for teachers.

Democratic mayors around the country have gone even further in their embrace of free market reforms. In June 2012, the US Conference of Mayors unanimously endorsed "parent trigger" laws pushed by the right that would, should a majority of parents vote in favor, allow public schools to fire teachers and further privatize schools by turning them over to private operators.[7] Antonio Villaraigosa, the Democratic mayor of Los Angeles, has publicly defended the parent trigger and pushed for near-total power over Los Angeles schools in order to institute corporate reforms with little public

---

7   Stephanie Simon, "Mayors Back Parents Seizing Control of Schools," *Reuters*, June 18, 2012. On the undemocratic premise underlying parent trigger laws, see Liza Featherstone, "'Empowerment' Against Democracy: Tinseltown and the Teachers' Unions," *Dissent*, September 26, 2012.

oversight—winning him support from then Republican Governor Arnold Schwarzenegger. Cory Booker, Democratic mayor of Newark, New Jersey, actually explicitly sided with his Republican governor, Chris Christie, on a similar policy agenda, including charter expansion and increased use of standardized test scores for teacher evaluations; he persuaded Facebook founder Mark Zuckerberg to donate $100 million to Newark schools to be used in an introduction of merit pay for teachers. The two Democratic mayors in charge in Chicago for the last quarter-century have also been national leaders in pushing a neoliberal education agenda.

Democrats have embraced the major philanthropic foundations and their agenda as well. Gates, for example, invested $90 million in Chicago's Renaissance 2010 program, which was overseen by former CEO of Chicago Public Schools Arne Duncan under Democratic Mayor Richard M. Daley. The program became the basis of the Obama administration's Race to the Top program, overseen by Duncan, who is now secretary of education. As education writer Joanne Barkan has said, Duncan made "the partnership with private foundations the defining feature of his [Department of Education] stewardship." In their foundation's annual report, Eli and Edythe Broad write:

[The] appointment of Arne Duncan . . . as the U.S. Secretary of Education marked the pinnacle of hope for our work in education reform. In many ways, we feel the stars have finally aligned. With an agenda that echoes our decades of investments—charter schools, performance

pay for teachers, accountability, expanded learning time,
and national standards—the Obama administration is
poised to cultivate and bring to fruition the seeds we and
other reformers have planted.

Duncan even created a director of philanthropic engagement
in the Department of Education—in his own words,
"signal[ling] to the philanthropic world that the Department
is 'open for business.'"[8]

From the very top of the national Democratic Party to the
local level, the consensus is unabashedly in favor of trans-
forming public education into a market commodity.

Chicago has long been what education policy scholar
Pauline Lipman describes as "incubator, test case, and model
for the neoliberal urban education agenda"—part of a larger
process of restructuring the city to better serve the needs of
capital. Since the 1990s, this has been marketed as education
reform. The 1995 Chicago School Reform Amendatory Act
put the mayor in full control of CPS, with the power to
appoint a school board and a CEO, and made an early push
for a more central role for high-stakes testing. Arne Duncan,
CEO of CPS under Richard M. Daley, crafted the Renaissance 2010 push. By 2009, ninety-two schools had been
designated as Ren2010 schools, and some three quarters of
them had been converted into charters. The program set up a
system of labeling and sorting schools in order to identify
those that were to be deemed failures—essentially setting

---

8   Barkan, "Got Dough?"

CPS up to become a portfolio manager of schools, obeying the logic of the market by determining which schools in its portfolio were failing and thus needed to be closed.[9]

Rahm Emanuel and the Board of Education have continued this push, particularly around school closures. In 2013, the board voted to shut down forty-nine elementary schools and a high school program—almost all of which are in African American neighborhoods—while the district continues to advance a plan to open sixty new charter schools. The combination of public school closings and charter school expansion will likely erode the union's membership, redirect public money to privately run charters that lack basic mechanisms for public accountability, slash teachers' salaries and benefits, and cause massive disruption in the neighborhoods where the closures would take place.

This agenda has been carried out in Chicago under total mayoral control, with almost no formal accountability to Chicagoans themselves. Ren2010 and the 2013 school closures might have been difficult to achieve if Chicago's mayors had to worry about public accountability. Writing about Chicago, "a national model of mayoral control," Lipman says, "Mayoral takeover is a case of the use of the coercive power of the state to enforce a neoliberal program."[10]

Chicago is perhaps the most Democratic of all American big cities, with a storied history of a political machine tied to that party. But it was also in the vanguard of the shift to a

---

9   Pauline Lipman, *The New Political Economy of Urban Education: Neoliberalism, Race, and the Right to the City*, Routledge, 2011.

10   Ibid., p. 61.

neoliberal managerial Democratic Party that aimed to placate new constituencies of capital rather than organized community interests or labor. That shift has seen education reform become synonymous with the free market and attacks on organized teachers.

Recognizing the Failure of Teachers Unions Nationally

The two major domestic teachers unions, the National Education Association and the American Federation of Teachers (AFT, of which the CTU is a member), have continually failed to even attempt to resist the Democratic Party's rightward shift on education. Even as the party is turning against them, they continue giving the Democrats millions of dollars—around $30 million in publicly disclosed donations and outside spending in the 2012 election cycle—seemingly expecting little in return.

There have been rumblings of a potential rupture in the teachers union–Democratic Party coalition for years, as teachers have grown increasingly agitated at the party's attacks on their profession. Indications of this have cropped up as more and more Democrats are becoming outspoken about their reticence or outright hostility toward teachers unions. Former Mayor Villaraigosa, for example, is not only a former union organizer but also a former *teachers union* organizer who now, lulled by the calls of the neoliberals, has turned on his former employer. Despite his claim that "I don't have an anti-union bone in my body," he wrote op-eds as mayor saying that although he has attempted to reform education, "there has been one unwavering roadblock to reform: *teacher union leadership* [emphasis in original]."[11]

Won't Back Down, a Hollywood film widely panned as little more than a teacher-slandering propaganda piece (and a godawful one, at that), was screened at the Democratic National Convention in 2012 (and, incidentally, given an introduction by Villaraigosa).[12] It was technically an unofficial event but one that required approval from the Obama White House. That a particularly noxious piece of antiunion and antieducator agitprop would be given the green light straight from the top, to be screened at the party's grand quadrennial event, says a great deal about how little the party seems to be concerned with maintaining even cordial relations with teachers unions.

In case teachers unions didn't get the message, President Obama's deputy campaign manager for the 2012 elections tweeted, in response to Republican sniping about the president being supposedly beholden to teachers unions, "Obama's relationship with teachers' unions [is] anything but cozy." It was a revealing statement: Democrats used to at least rhetorically claim their deep commitment to organized labor while betraying it behind closed doors; in the era of neoliberal education consensus, all such pretensions appear to have vanished.

---

11 Antonio Villaraigosa, "It Is Time for Teachers Unions to Join the Education Reform Team," *Huffington Post*, December 7, 2010. Stan Wilson, "L.A. Mayor Backs Weighing Student Performance in Evaluating Teacher Quality," CNN, September 12, 2012.
12 Frank Bruni, "Teachers on the Defensive," *New York Times*, June 27, 2010.

The message from Democrats has been fairly clear: Teachers unions are no longer a needed constituency within the Democratic coalition, so it's now open season where they are concerned.

Yet neither of the national unions appears capable of fighting back. The NEA has recently responded by beginning to fund some Republicans, like a state house candidate in Indiana who hadn't spent much time on charter expansion or merit pay because he had been busy with bills to ban gay marriage and hunt down undocumented immigrants, or the Pennsylvania state representative who bragged that the voter identification law he helped craft would deliver his state to Mitt Romney in the election.

The AFT has not started handing out cash to conservatives, but it has not changed its interactions with the Democrats either. Its president, Randi Weingarten, is of specific interest because she has positioned herself as one of the principal voices in education nationally. (A *New York Times* columnist even floated her name for secretary of education soon after the CTU strike.)[13] Weingarten has, in the words of education reporter Dana Goldstein, "tried to carve out a conciliatory role for herself in the national debate over education policy." In doing so, she has ceded much ground to the reformers' agenda. Goldstein called her the "marker of the moving center"—a center unquestionably shifting far to the right.[14]

---

13   Joe Nocera, "Obama's New Cabinet," *New York Times*, November 26, 2012.
14   Dana Goldstein, "The Education Wars," *American Prospect*, March 20, 2009.

In July 2012, for example, Weingarten praised a contract negotiated in Cleveland that introduced teacher evaluations based on standardized test scores before considering either seniority or tenure. She held up a contract negotiated in Newark, New Jersey, that introduced merit pay (paid for with a $100 million donation by Facebook founder Mark Zuckerberg, and specifically designated to institute the kinds of changes trumpeted by corporate reformers) as "a system of the future . . . that will help boost teaching and learning and will strengthen the teaching profession." In 2010, she publicly supported a Colorado bill that went further in stripping teachers of tenure protections than any other piece of legislation in the nation in order to make the state more competitive in its bid for Race to the Top funds.[15]

And perhaps most jarringly, Weingarten actually came to Chicago on the first day teachers began voting to authorize the strike—not in support of teachers but to speak on the Clinton Global Initiative panel alongside Rahm Emanuel and to praise him for his Chicago Infrastructure Trust, a privatized infrastructure project that is a huge coup for capital.[16] So

15   Cleveland: Lee Sustar, "Can the AFT Meet the Challenge?" *Socialist Worker*, July 25, 2012. Newark: Josh Eidelson, "Newark Teachers Union Embraces Performance Pay, Wins Peer Review," *In These Times*, October 22, 2012; Devin Leonard, "Facebook and the Newark Schools: About that $100 Million . . ." *BusinessWeek*, June 28, 2012; "Newark, N.J., Teachers Ratify Contract," American Federation of Teachers, November 14, 2012.
16   "Dynamic Duo: Randi Weingarten and Rahm Emanuel—CGI America 2012," YouTube. On the Infrastructure Trust and its implications for infrastructure projects and the public sphere, see Ramsin Canon, "It's Not the Privatization, It's the Privatization," *Gapers Block*, April 16, 2012, gapersblock.com.

while Chicago's teachers were engaging in a historic strike vote to push back against free market education reform, Weingarten was ignoring them and supporting a neoliberal mayor in chipping away at public infrastructure.

These policies and stances come from Weingarten's view of what effective union leadership looks like.

"You may look heroic when you yell at people," Weingarten told Goldstein, "but if you actually find ways to really work together and reach across the aisle, that's what I want."

Weingarten hints at a labor-management cooperation scheme that has been tried and has failed too many times to count, both from a left perspective and on its own terms, throughout American labor history—not only because it is based on a misunderstanding of the opposed interests of the two groups but also because it can no longer deliver the goods for workers. American union leaders have pushed such arrangements particularly zealously since the 1980s, although this did not slow the decline in living standards of unionized workers and the American working class as a whole.

The unspoken hope is that labor leaders will begin to identify more with the bosses they are negotiating against than with the workers they represent—draining leaders and their members of any sort of fighting spirit. American labor history shows that such arrangements inevitably presage new attacks and demands for concessions from bosses—something much easier to accomplish when the union leadership is in league with the perpetrators of the attacks.

There is either a naïveté about the nature of the project Weingarten and all teachers unions are up against or an unwillingness to come to terms with it. Education reformers want nothing less than the dismantlement of education as a public good and the ability to reshape it to the dictates of the market. There is no room for teachers unions in this view of education—at least not teachers unions that have any meaningful power over the decisions being made in the education system. The only way to effectively respond to this project is to challenge it head-on, to identify it as detrimental and fight against it unapologetically—and to put forward teachers' own vision of what progressive education reform can look like.

Up Against the Democrats

Central to the task of pushing back against the free market reform agenda was taking on the party that embraced it so fully—the Democrats. The previous union leadership, the UPC, was neither willing nor able to challenge the neoliberal consensus on education in Chicago, as discussed in Chapter 2. The opposite is true of CORE: Years before it even considered running for control of the union, teacher activists were battling the local and national Democratic education agenda.

A battle against the Democratic Party was actually not such a big leap for CTU members, as two decades of policies attacking public education had produced a clear desire among much of the membership to fight the party.

"No one in the union had been happy about the Democrats on education, locally or nationally," Jesse Sharkey said. "So rather than it being a big shift, we essentially just acknowledged what most of our members already thought."

As President Obama's chief of staff, Rahm Emanuel in response to concerns about autoworkers under the auto industry bailout, once stated, "Fuck the UAW." Since then, he has proven during his mayoral tenure to have no qualms about inserting the name of any other union at the end of that phrase—the CTU included or perhaps especially. The soil had been tilled before him: School closures and the expansion of nonunion charters had lost the union some six thousand members. But union leadership at that point had still been unwilling and unable to take on Richard M. Daley, who for much of his tenure as mayor had quieted the rank and file by negotiating economically generous contracts with the CTU.

In contrast, ever since he took office in 2011, the union has named Emanuel as a primary target. He was "clearly anti-teacher from the very beginning," according to Karen Lewis. In an interview, Lewis quoted Emanuel as having said that a quarter of CPS students were "never going to make it and that he wasn't going to throw money at the problem." At another time, she also said that "I don't think he really cares about poor people, people of color." A journalist profiling Lewis opined that she was "willing to publicly and rather starkly characterize the battle with the mayor over education reform as a kind of class war."[17]

---

17   "Karen Lewis on the 'Ed Show': Rahm Is 'Absolutely' Anti-Teacher," *Huffington Post*, October 11, 2011; Ben Goldberger, "Karen Lewis, Street Fighter," *Chicago*, November 2012.

This kind of oppositional language had rarely been heard from union officials in Chicago, in teachers unions or elsewhere. It painted a clear picture for the public: Rahm Emanuel did not believe in expending resources on a huge percentage of the poor children of color that make up the CPS; the Chicago Teachers Union did.

Emanuel quickly became a strong target of loathing by teachers. Anti-Emanuel chants rang off the downtown highrises every day during the strike, and teachers' picket signs were filled with invective against him.

All that is wrong with American education reform should not be placed solely on the shoulders of Rahm Emanuel; his policies reflect a larger free market consensus that must be challenged. And there is always a danger in holding up a single politician as the primary enemy to be defeated. But the union's decision to target Emanuel specifically represents a significant break in union–Democratic Party relations, both in Chicago and nationally: The CTU was unafraid to name a major national power player in the Democratic Party as an enemy and therefore to go to battle with him over his support of neoliberal reforms.

Like its mayors, Chicago's city council members or aldermen are Democrats through and through: forty-nine of the council's fifty members belong to the party. And like their national party, they seem to have strong right-wing currents throughout their ranks. Days before the strike, nearly two thirds of the council signed a letter to Karen Lewis begging the union not to go out on strike.

Some signatories, like Alderman Joe Moreno, went

further—during an interview on Fox Business News, Moreno agreed with a host who suggested that the city "blow up the traditional schools and have more charter schools." He then stated, "We're trying to reform education. Any time we talk about reforming education—doing charter schools, doing turnaround schools, which I totally support—we get push-back from the Chicago Teachers Union. They're a conservative union."[18]

Moreno portrays himself as a progressive council member, but he is of that peculiar brand of twenty-first-century liberalism that does not include supporting workers on strike and encourages expansion of the market into public education. Thus, after teachers and activists highlighted Moreno's comments, rank-and-file CTU members confronted the alderman directly with pickets in front of his office, organizing actions independently of the union. (Since then, the alderman—likely rattled by the mobilization against him after his comments—has attempted to make amends with the union and other grassroots groups throughout the city.) Other ostensibly progressive city council members who opposed the strike (like Joe Moore, an alderman once named the "Most Valuable Local Official" by *The Nation*) faced similar actions throughout the city.

The union has even taken on what is a sacred cow for most American unions: President Obama. The CTU did not vote to endorse Obama's reelection campaign for president, an uncommon move for any American union. The political

18   Joe Macare, "Hipster Alderman Agrees With Fox Host: 'Blow Up' Chicago Schools," *Occupied Chicago Tribune*, September 12, 2012, occupiedchicagotribune.org.

action committee voted to endorse his reelection campaign, but a contentious debate on the floor of the House of Delegates resulted in no action on an Obama endorsement.

The strike itself was timed to present a political crisis for the president. As the presidential campaign approached a fever pitch less than two months before the presidential elections, the teachers walked off the job in Obama's hometown, causing a minor crisis for the president that could have escalated if the strike had dragged on. And while it was not made explicit during the strike, the CTU was fighting policies that were central to Obama's education reform agenda.

The president's signature education legislation is Race to the Top, a federal competitive-grants-based program that is largely based on Renaissance 2010, encouraging school turnarounds, increased use of standardized testing to evaluate teachers, and merit pay. The union successfully prevented the Board of Education from introducing merit pay in Chicago and pushed to reduce the proportion of a teacher's evaluation based on standardized tests to its legal minimum. Halting turnarounds and closures is now the central piece of the union's agenda.

And during the national convention of the AFT in July 2012, as Vice President Joe Biden addressed them, CTU members in red shirts stood on the floor of their national union's convention handing out fliers to other members and holding signs reading "Stop Race to the Top." CTU President Karen Lewis was the only member of the AFT's executive council who did not sit on the convention's stage during Biden's address, seen in videos and photos from the event, standing on the convention floor with her arms crossed.[19]

While most American unions have been terrified to break with any sections of the Democratic Party, even those pushing neoliberal policies that are throwing those unions' very existence into question, the CTU has not. That willingness was key to its ability to win its strike and build power.

Targeting Billionaires

While the push for free market education reform is a project with clear intentions of eradicating teachers unions in order to reshape education according to the dictates of capital, few teachers unions have been willing to publicly identify it as such—or to identify as their enemy the wealthy capitalists who are pushing it. The CTU, however, has been willing to unequivocally identify neoliberal education reformers as enemies of public education. Thus the CTU has put the issues at stake in efforts to reform public education in stark contrast—and made clear whose side the ultrarich reformers are on.

A widely circulated video entitled "Chicago Teachers Union vs. Astroturf Billionaires" was indicative of the union's willingness to isolate and attack the billionaire reformers, highlighting the personal and ideological ties between Mayors Richard Daley and Rahm Emanuel, corporate reform groups

---

19   George Schmidt, "AFT Reports: Chicago Played Major role in the American Federation of Teachers Convention in 2012," *Substance News*, August 1, 2012, substancenews.net.

like Stand for Children and Democrats for Education Reform, and far-right groups affiliated with the Tea Party. Another video included a mock-children's cartoon, telling a "bedtime story" of the "fat cats" who had attacked the teachers and attempted to pillage the public school system in Chicago. The video goes as far as describing "a new evil fat cat land[ing] in Chicago," Emanuel, who flashes across the screen as a devilish-looking cat, who "brought in a whole litter box of evil fat cats from all over the country." Meanwhile, caricatures of other nefarious-looking cats appear, representing Stand for Children, billionaire Bruce Rauner, and others.

Rauner, a retired private equity fund manager who has taken up the dismantling of public education as a hobby in the way many retirees take up golf, began to emerge as a prominent voice around education reform during the strike. A close adviser to Mayor Emanuel, Rauner is a strong backer of charter schools—his donations to a prominent local charter network resulted in his name being affixed to a school in the city's West Loop, now called Rauner College Prep. He frequently appears in public to attack the union and was responsible for bringing Stand for Children to Illinois in 2011. (SfC would later go on to pass SB7, as described in Chapter 2.)

The union has confronted Rauner publicly. Karen Lewis wrote an op-ed in the *Chicago Tribune* addressing Rauner specifically, concluding, "Obviously he knows absolutely nothing about education." And shortly after the strike's end, Jesse Sharkey sat next to Rauner on a local news broadcast and calmly argued that wealthy reformers like Rauner were actually pushing public education's decline through their attacks on teachers and collective bargaining.[20] Sharkey stated:

> It's ironic to hear someone who's a billionaire, whose interests in the schools aren't based in his longstanding work in that school system, talk about how what's ruining the schools [is] the very people who go into those schools every day and pour their heart and soul into the public education system. . . . Frankly, if you want to know what's wrong with the public education system, it's been a series of efforts of corporate, top-down reform that don't take the opinions of the actual educators into account.

At one time billionaires like Rauner and corporate reform groups like Stand for Children could make their case for free market education reforms unopposed; if teachers unions had any kind of response to the accusations leveled against them, they were often mealy-mouthed, reinforcing the narrative that wealthy reformers were pushing changes while teachers unions acted as roadblocks. The CTU has changed the narrative on education reform in

---

20   Chicago Schools Forward, "Stand Up to the Fat Cats," December 9, 2012, YouTube; Karen Lewis, "Karen Lewis Takes Aim at a Critic of CPS Teachers," *Chicago Tribune*, September 14, 2012; "Mayor's Adviser Attacks CTU," *Chicago Tonight*, WTTW, September 19, 2012. video.wttw.com/video/2280999377/.

Chicago, both in media portrayals and in the minds of CPS parents.

If more teachers unions were willing to make their case directly to the public—that the wealthy capitalists funding education reform efforts in this country are acting against the interests of public school students and must be stopped, as the CTU has done—what passes for education reform in this country could see a marked shift.

Proposing Positive Policy Visions

The union members would not have been able to position themselves as the true representatives of the interests of Chicago's public school students if they had not been willing to articulate an alternative vision for what Chicago public schools should look like. In February 2012, the union released "The Schools Chicago's Students Deserve: Research-based Proposals to Strengthen Elementary and Secondary Education in the Chicago Public Schools." This forty-six-page white paper rebukes education reform as it has been carried out in CPS and nationally and lays out the union's vision for education reform. This vision includes an unapologetic shoring up of education as a public good that gives no credence to any of the free market or high-stakes-testing-obsessed schemes in vogue in the mainstream education reform dialogue.

The report's first sentence reads, "Every student in CPS deserves to have the same quality education as the children of the wealthy." It demands smaller class sizes, stronger and better-staffed "wraparound services" like nurses and social workers, and the provision of basic facilities like libraries in all schools. It cites the widespread overburdening of special education teachers and argues for additional resources for their students. It directly challenges what it refers to as the "pedagogy of poverty," the transformation of teaching into a practice largely focused on preparation for standardized testing. Recognizing the very real crisis in many poor schools, the report demands additional funding for such schools rather than closures.

And in a welcome departure from much of twenty-first-century liberalism, the document rejects the logic of austerity, which justifies the underfunding of public resources by pleading budget shortfalls. It is unapologetic in the audaciousness of its demands, proposing funding for these proposals through tax increases for the rich, progressive tax policies (including an end to the regressive practice of school funding based on property taxes), a financial transactions tax, and an overhaul of the TIF system that has taken millions from public institutions like schools and funneled them to corporations.

The paper is the union's public response to both the corporate reform agenda and teachers unions' grudging capitulation to it. It is a proposal that cedes no ground to the neoliberals and advances its own agenda for school reform. While the CTU is on the defensive overall, as nearly all unions currently are, its policy proposals for education reform are a labor movement rarity: a union attempting to reshape public discourse by advancing its own vision for what society should look like. Most unions do not move past the defensive crouch they are forced into by bosses on the attack and politicians pushing austerity. The CTU is insisting that the union and its members know what the American education system should look like; at a time of labor's timidity, they are making steps toward going on the offensive.

Collective Bargaining for the Common Good

The CTU had made gains for students a central part of its public rhetoric around its fight with the mayor and the Board of Education and a core reason for the strike. At the bargaining table, however, the union also negotiated gains that extended far beyond teachers' compensation. It employed what labor strategist Stephen Lerner has called "collective bargaining connected to the common good."[21]

A key provision of SB7 was to significantly limit the scope of legally strikeable issues for teachers. Under the law, teachers could strike only over wages, benefits, and some aspects of evaluation. This provision was pursued by the union's enemies because they recognized the union's potential to use the strike as a referendum on the state of public education as a whole and, particularly under the union's new left leadership, as a weapon to extract contractual gains on noncompensation issues that affect students.

---

21 Stephen Lerner, "An Injury to All: Going Beyond Collective Bargaining As We Have Known It," *New Labor Forum*, Spring 2010.

That these neoliberal groups would not only attempt to outlaw a strike but also keep a strike's legality limited to extremely narrow parameters is an explicit recognition of Lerner's argument: "Expanding the goals and demands of organizing and collective bargaining is the key to winning individual campaigns, a stronger labor movement, and a more just society." In effect, groups like SfC recognized not only that teachers' ability to withhold their labor was a powerful weapon but also that a strike which made an issue of the conditions under which children were being educated would be extremely difficult to discredit and defeat.

Mutually Beneficial Achievements

Yet the union did expand its goals and demands during the strike. It took the proposals it had put forward in documents like "The Schools Chicago's Children Deserve" and made noncompensation issues a key piece of its case to the public and a central matter in its 2012 strike (despite the fact that the latter was illegal). Even in the union's press release announcing the work stoppage, President Karen Lewis said the strike was about "getting a fair contract which will give our students the resources they deserve." Outside the union's headquarters the night before the strike, Lewis said, "As we continue to bargain in good faith, we stand in solidarity with parents, clergy, and community-based organizations who are advocating for smaller class sizes, a better school day, and an elected school board." The union maintained this message without running afoul of the law.

And these concerns were not mere rhetoric. The union actually did use its bargaining position to win real gains for students in its contract.

Nearly six hundred new art, music, and gym teachers were to be added to the teaching force—a particularly critical gain in a school system where, at the elementary level, for example, only 25 percent of neighborhood schools had both art and music teachers. For the first time, textbooks were guaranteed on the first day of class—many teachers throughout the city had actually begun previous years without them. The board was attempting to negotiate the elimination of class size caps; the union not only kept such caps in place but won $500,000 to attempt to reduce class sizes. A committee was created and allotted another $500,000 to hire additional special education teachers.[22] The union even negotiated an increase in a classroom supply budget of 150 percent.

Beyond negotiating contract provisions that were beneficial mostly to students, the union successfully made the strike about American education reform. They made the obsession with standardized testing a subject for debate—a direct challenge to both the right and the Obama administration's education policy, as Race to the Top expands the use of standardized testing in evaluating teachers' effectiveness. The union successfully pushed for a hiring pool for teachers who had been laid off through no fault of their own; 50

---

22   The long-term viability of several of these contract demands, such as negotiating smaller class sizes and hiring new teachers, has been thrown into question, however, as CPS carried out massive budget cuts and teacher layoffs in the lead-up to the 2013 school year.

percent of new hires must come from that pool. As a result, CPS cannot remove longtime teachers at will in order to replace them with younger, cheaper teachers. This provision will help to reduce the constant churn of teachers that is seen at the city's charter schools, which puts an inexperienced workforce at the helm of classrooms throughout the city. The union made a central issue of the declining numbers of educators of color in a school district that has over 90 percent students of color, thus defending both educators and students of color within the schools as well showing a larger willingness to name CPS's policies as deeply racist and promoting "educational apartheid."

Highlighting Racial Justice

Education reformers have openly addressed the undeniable fact of the miserable conditions for poor public school students of color around the country. After the Department of Education released data showing massive educational inequality in US schools, Secretary of Education Arne Duncan stated, "The undeniable truth is that the everyday educational experience for many students of color violates the principle of equity at the heart of the American promise. It is our collective duty to change that." While some of their ideological ilk have been loathe to even mention the existence of racial inequality, Duncan and other neoliberal reformers have explicitly and effectively positioned themselves as *the* defenders of communities of color while also often positioning themselves against the teachers unions, whom they portray as defenders of the status quo and thus of racial inequality. For the most part, teachers unions have stood by idly as reformers like Duncan appropriated the mantle of the civil rights movement.

The reluctance to name and attack racist schooling policies while racial inequalities have widened and parents have waged fights against them has created a vacuum into which neoliberal education reformers have stepped. Reformers have only been able to portray themselves as inheritors of the legacy of the mid-twentieth-century civil rights movement because teachers unions have not. While not all parent and community groups accept the reformers' claims at face value, those who do can hardly be faulted: Reformers are appealing to communities' deep desires to change a schooling system that has failed them for decades.

The problem stretches far back. While teachers unions have supported community-led struggles for racial justice throughout their history, they have too often been actively hostile to them. An example is the teachers strike in the Ocean Hill–Brownsville section of Brooklyn in 1968, when black community groups entered into open battle with AFT locals on strike. Today, there is no street fighting between black parent activists and teachers union members, but there is little active support by the latter of the former's struggles. Most teachers unions do little to actively embrace the causes of community groups fighting for racial justice in public schools and would never describe the conditions in urban public schools around the country as "like apartheid," despite the overwhelming evidence that this is the case. Even progressive-minded union locals are afraid to push their membership on the issues of racial inequality, and they would never want to engage in genuine power-sharing with community organizations that might push them to take risks that don't sit well with union staff.

The CTU is one of the few teachers union locals around the country willing to name the policies of its district—in which 91.2 percent of students are students of color, 87 percent are poor students, and 90 percent attend schools classified as "hypersegregated"—as racist. In speeches, policy papers, and statements to the press, the union has described Chicago's schools as "apartheid-like." In a June 2013 speech at the City Club of Chicago, Karen Lewis said, "Rich white people think they know what's in the best interests of children of African-Americans and Latinos. . . . There's something about these folks who use little black and brown children as stage props at one press conference while announcing they want to fire, lay off, or lock up their parents at another."[23]

The union has supported community groups in filing Title VI civil rights complaints with the Department of Education's Office of Civil Rights around school turnarounds and closures in black and Latino neighborhoods. Its November 2012 report in particular, titled "The Black and White of Education in Chicago," attacks CPS for exacerbating racial inequality by examining the racial composition of neighborhoods and

23   Ted Cox, "CTU's Karen Lewis Blames 'Rich White People' for Education Inequity," *DNAInfo.com*, June 18, 2013.

schools targeted for closures and turnarounds; it points out that the larger a school's population of students of color, the more likely it is to be shuttered. Since 2001, some 88 percent of CPS students who have been affected by closures or turnarounds have been African American.

Teachers of color have long been the ones willing to work in these hypersegregated conditions. But according to the union's data, the percentage of black teachers in CPS has declined from 45 percent in 1995 to 29 percent in 2011, leading to a lawsuit filed in late 2012 against the district by three fired black teachers and the union. The steep decline in the number of teachers of color in CPS schools has serious implications for the black "middle class" in Chicago as well as for students of color; as it organized in the years before the 2010 election, CORE agitated around this issue and has made it a central organizing task since taking office.

Brandon Johnson was once a middle school reading and social studies teacher and is now an organizer for the union. He realized the extent to which black teachers were under attack in Chicago through his conversations with activists who had fought for black teachers to become full members of the union and full employees of the CPS during the Civil Rights era. A retired teacher who had witnessed the struggles to bring black teachers into full membership in the union told him, "This is in direct retaliation to what we built in the '60s and '70s. They're trying to kill you."

"I was really livid," Johnson said, "to think that there was a system that does not value an entire race of teachers—especially when 90 percent of students are students of color, and a good portion of them black."

The union's Black Teachers Caucus was an independent rank-and-file organization that agitated against the conservative union's leadership during the Civil Rights and Black Power eras, fighting for both improvements in black students' learning conditions and the betterment of black teachers, most of whom had been limited to being "full-time basis substitutes."[24] In order to continue that fight, Johnson helped restart a Black Caucus—which he now heads.

The union has made the issue of racial inequality central to its day-to-day work in a way that speaks to the concerns of both teachers of color and parents in communities of color whose children bear the brunt of decades of disinvestment in their schools and neighborhoods. By doing so, they have wrested the banner of racial justice and the trust of communities of color out of the hands of the neoliberals in Chicago.

Social Movement Unionism in American Labor

Most American unions have long seen their central task as the defense of their members' interests. This contrasts sharply with unions throughout the rest of the world, many of which see themselves as defenders of the interests of the working class as a whole. Labor scholar Kim Moody describes the two models—business   unionism   versus   social   movement

---

24   John F. Lyons gives an account of the history of this and other racial justice struggles within the union in *Teachers and Reform: Chicago Public Education, 1929–70*, University of Illinois Press, 2008.

unionism: "The former's vision does not extend beyond 'bread-and-butter' issues related to workers' compensation; the latter identifies itself as a vehicle for society-wide transformation on issues that affect communities beyond individual workplaces."[25]

The tension between those two visions has been present since the birth and throughout the history of American teacher unionism. Since its earliest days, liberal and radical members have attempted to push unions' agendas to the left, toward a unionism that defends public education and fights for progressive reform; conservative unionists have stuck to fighting over compensation and have largely won out.

Social movement unionism that aims to push a broadly transformative agenda for all should be pursued because it is, from a left perspective, the proper thing to do. But for labor as a whole and teachers unions in particular, the experience of the CTU shows that it is also the *only* thing to do. Teacher unionism cannot survive the attacks it is currently facing by neoliberal education reformers without answering those attacks head-on, taking up an agenda that both defends teachers *and* fights for students' and communities' best interests through a defense of public education.

Just as conservative business unionism and liberal reform unionism has failed to "bring home the whole hog" for members in contract fights over the last decades, so have they failed to help create broad movements for justice that engage

25 Kim Moody, *U.S. Labor in Trouble and Transition: The Failure of Reform from Above, The Promise of Revival from Below*, Verso, 2008.

the working class beyond unionized workers. Teacher's unions' fates in the twenty-first century will rest on their ability to represent the concerns of the students, parents, and communities they serve while arguing forcefully that free market forces do not serve these groups. Anything less will be suicide.

CONCLUSION

In May 2011, in the lead-up to the Chicago teachers strike, Mayor Rahm Emanuel appointed Jean-Claude Brizard, a former teacher and schools administrator in New York City and Rochester, to be CEO of Chicago Public Schools (CPS). Brizard would last less than a year and a half in the position. He was brought in as it became clear that the city's teachers would be striking for the first time in a generation and then dismissed (with a $250,000 severance package) a month after teachers and parents had treated him as the political punching bag he was clearly intended to be.

Brizard remained quiet for nearly a year after leaving Chicago, but in August 2013 he sat down with an education think tank to discuss his tenure.

When asked about his interactions with the CTU, Brizard said, "We severely underestimated the ability of the Chicago Teachers Union to lead a massive grassroots campaign against our administration. It's a lesson for all of us in the reform community."[1]

---

1   Alex Parker, "Jean-Claude Brizard: We 'Underestimated' Teachers Union," *DNAInfo.com*, August 22, 2013.

There are few times in recent American history when unions have surprised anyone—bosses, the public, the broader left, even their own members. The typical sentiment is closer to labor lawyer Tom Geoghegan's in the opening words to his memoir *Which Side Are You On?*: "'Organized labor.' Say those words, and your heart sinks . . . It is a dumb, stupid mastodon of a thing." Most twenty-first-century unions don't teach anyone many lessons—to many, it is a wonder they have not gone extinct.

The CTU has transformed itself into an organization that no one could call mastodonic. It is a union whose power is undeniable, even to a former CEO with whom it had only recently done battle. And it is a union that could and should serve as an example to all workers, whose latent power within the American and worldwide economy goes underestimated and unused each day.

Nationally, strike levels are at all-time lows. Every decade since the 1970s the number of strikes undertaken by workers has steadily diminished; it might be an exaggeration to state that today the strike is nearly extinct, but not by much. The number of workdays lost to strikes in the post–World War II period, labor's heyday, was 60 million; in 2010, it was 180,000.[2]

Those numbers have largely mirrored the decline of labor's membership since the onset of deindustrialization. Over the last four decades, as the movement's membership

---

2   Doug Henwood, "Strike Wave!" *Left Business Observer*, August 18, 2010.

has declined and as attacks on unions and the public sphere have increased, unions have responded not with a renewed resolve to push back against those attacks but by scaling back their struggle. But this strategy has failed. Capital has ratcheted up its offensive against labor and expects little resistance in response. By contrast, the unionism pushed by the CTU since the election of the Caucus of Rank-and-File Educators (CORE) has rejected the strategy of accommodation, of capitulation, and of ceding the terms of debate over education reform and the idea of the public sector as a whole to labor's enemies.

Mainstream media coverage of teachers unions and public sector unions in general has given many—even those on the left and those working in the labor movement—the impression that public sector workers' fights are uphill battles against a public duped into believing that such unions are their enemy. There are some data to support this claim; since the 1980s, public opinion of public sector unions has grown less and less favorable. But the CTU showed that such declines are not inevitable. The public can be won over to the public workers' side—not despite striking, but actually *through* striking.

That is not to say, however, that unions can bring about a revitalized labor movement by simply engaging in more strikes. Radicals often fetishize workers' use of the strike, seeming to believe that any problem workers confront can be solved by withholding their labor. But in the case of the CTU, the strike was part of a broader fight against neoliberal education reform. Its fight was based on a broad vision of what progressive education reform could look like; it included genuine organizing alongside communities and public demonstrations over issues beyond teachers' bread-and-butter concerns, such as provisions beneficial to students. Placing the strike within the framework of a larger strategy allowed Chicago's teachers to win.

CORE has become part of a long history in the American labor movement of disillusioned rank-and-file union members rebelling against conservative leadership, many through similar caucuses and other independent groups.[3] Today, varying levels of democracy are available to disgruntled union militants looking to shake up their unions. Some locals, like the CTU, have fairly open internal structures that can be effectively used by well-organized activists. In others, however, that is not the case. In the United Federation of Teachers (UFT) in New York City, for example, retired union members loyal to the old guard make up over half the votes in leadership elections—making challenges by the rank-and-file nearly impossible. Within many of the Service Employees International Union (SEIU)'s "megalocals," which often span multiple states and include tens of thousands or even hundreds of thousands of members, it is difficult to imagine a group of rank-and-file workers successfully challenging their leadership.[4] Whatever a

3   Aaron Brenner, Robert Brenner, and Cal Winslow, eds., *Rebel Rank and File: Labor Militancy and Revolt from Below During the Long 1970s*, Verso, 2010.

4   New York: Sarah Butrymowicz, "In Retirees, UFT Leadership Finds

union's structure and level of democracy, there are bodies of knowledge built up over years of struggle that aspiring dissidents can access. Most notable among these is the publication *Labor Notes* and the organization behind it, which helped the members of CORE and amplified their message as they slowly began to form a caucus. It has been the most prominent American labor organization in working with radical unionists. Since the end of its strike, the CTU itself has taken its message on the road to union workers of all occupations, sharing its story with both rank-and-file activists and progressive union leadership throughout the country.

Even among labor's ostensibly progressive wings, internal democracy and leadership development of rank-and-file workers has never been much of a priority. And for good reason from union bureaucrats' point of view: union leaders—whether progressive, centrist, or reactionary—worry that their power will be challenged by savvy dissidents. In many cases, their fears are well-founded. But if social movement unionism of the sort that the CTU has pursued under CORE is to spread throughout the labor movement, agitation and organizing by independent groups of rank-and-file union members will be essential.

There is no single way out of the slump that teachers unions and the broader labor movement—the institutions tasked with defending the working class as a whole—find themselves in. But revitalization will not be found by

Loyal—and Unusual—Support," *GothamSchools.org*, March 12, 2013.

continuing the failed strategy of conservative, parochial, top-down unionism. The CTU developed its membership in a way it had never done before, and it was willing to expand its concerns to students and communities beyond its members' own. By the time teachers took the militant step of walking off the job, they were striking for the future of public education and in defense of the entire working class—and they won. If the entire working class is to win, its defenders should take note.

After the Strike

Since September 2012, other unions in Chicago and elsewhere have seemed to take some inspiration from Chicago teachers. The leadership of the American Federation of State, County and Municipal Employees Council 31, which represents 75,000 public sector workers in Illinois, publicly praised the CTU's strike and came close to striking themselves in a contract battle with Governor Pat Quinn, a Democrat. Some half dozen teachers union locals near Chicago have themselves gone on strike since the CTU strike, with mixed results in contract negotiations.

The SEIU Local 1, a massive property-services local spanning multiple states, has ratcheted up its rhetoric against Mayor Rahm Emanuel in contract and layoff fights—a fact of note both because confrontation with the Democratic Party is rare in the American labor movement and because SEIU has positioned itself as *the* key backer of the Democratic Party nationally, spending more, for example, on President

Obama's reelection campaign than any other entity.[5]

Rank-and-file activism among teachers and all unions is seeing an uptick. After its leadership negotiated a contract that included the introduction of merit pay, the Newark Education Workers Caucus, in Newark, New Jersey, was formed. The fact that its members take inspiration from the CTU has led the union's president to state, "They had some signs there that we should follow Chicago's lead. . . . I think that's very dangerous." In New York City, the Movement of Rank and File Educators (MORE) formed among United Federation of Teachers members. The UFT has been the home base for the leadership of the American Federation of Teachers (AFT)—including current president Randi Weingarten, a former UFT president—since the 1960s, and the Unity Caucus has ruled uninterrupted for the duration. Although MORE lost its electoral challenge to the caucus in April 2013, it has vowed to continue to push the UFT from the left and will likely run again in future elections. Outside of education, rank-and-file nurses in New York, graduate students in California, longshore workers in Alabama, and Teamsters in New York City, among many others, have run reform slates in their unions in recent years and won.[6]

---

5   Kari Lydersen, "Rahm the Grinch? Janitors Say Emanuel Is Stealing Their Christmas," *In These Times*, December 12, 2012: Melanie Trottman and Brody Mullins, "Union Is Top Spender for Democrats," *Wall Street Journal*, November 1, 2012.
6   Newark: Josh Eidelson, "Some Newark Teachers, Inspired by Chicago, Seek to Thwart Concessionary Contract," *In These Times*, October 26, 2012: Samantha Winslow, "Newark Teacher Reformers Win Majority," *Labor Notes*, June 26, 2013. New York: Sarah Jaffe, "New York Didn't Pull

Beyond elections, teachers unions are seeing some signs of militancy alongside communities. The Philadelphia Federation of Teachers, decimated by shock-doctrine–style reforms over recent years, has formed a citywide coalition with parents and other community groups to try to halt school closures and educator layoffs, and has released a report similar to the CTU's articulating their own vision of what school reform should look like. Rank-and-file teachers from Garfield High School in Seattle voted almost unanimously to boycott a standardized test, alongside the school's Parent Teacher Association, despite the high stakes attached to that action. Another Seattle school soon joined them, and then the boycott spread to schools in Portland, Denver, and New York City. While both the National Education Association and the AFT have issued statements and resolutions against standardized testing, it is rank-and-file teachers who have taken the steps to actually refuse to administer them.[7]

Tepidly, some unions have begun to break with

---

a Chicago but Dissident Teachers Aren't Giving up," *In These Times*, April 26, 2013. Nationwide: Mark Brenner, "Reformers Resurgent? A Survey of Recent Rank-and-File Uprisings," *New Labor Forum*, Spring 2013.

7   Valerie Strauss, "Philadelphia to Close 23 Public Schools; Randi Weingarten Arrested at Protest," *Washington Post*, March 7, 2013; Samantha Winslow, "Philadelphia Teachers Take School Closings Fight Citywide," *Labor Notes*, February 14, 2013; "Excellent Schools for All Children: The Philadelphia Community Education Plan," Philadelphia Coalition Advocating for Public Schools, December 2012. The case of the Philadelphia teachers union is especially indicative of the level of attacks teachers unions are currently facing. The demands the union is facing from the Philadelphia School District are stunning in their audacity. See Kristen Graham, "No Seniority? No Water Fountains? More on the Contract," *Philadelphia Inquirer*, February 27, 2013. Seattle: Jackie Micucci, "How Garfield High Defeated the MAP Test," *Seattle*, August 2013.

the Democratic Party's more explicitly neoliberal wing. Moreover, opposition to free market education reform and a willingness to strike is clearly spreading among teachers unions everywhere—in part because of the example the CTU has given of what an effective militant struggle can look like.

But unions should not oversimplify the CTU's example. Reviving the strike, as Joe Burns argued in his 2011 book, will be key for labor to revive itself. But it will not help if more unions simply walk off the job, particularly in education and the public sector broadly, where strikes interrupt the provision of services that are critically needed by working-class people; that is not a viable strategy for future victories. It is not enough for unions generally and public sector unions in particular to simply stop production or service provision; they must figure out, as the CTU did, how to effectively utilize work stoppages as focal points that can rally community support (and, one hopes, the support of other unions) for a larger movement against neoliberal reform.[8]

Indeed, CORE's raison d'être was not centered around the old union leadership's unwillingness to strike, even though the United Progressive Caucus (UPC) had not led the union out on strike in a generation. Rather, neighborhood public schools throughout the city were continually being shuttered, with charter schools springing up in their wake, under the neoliberal education agenda pushed by the mayor and the head of CPS. The policies were serious blows to Chicago teachers and students alike, providing a potential opening for

8   This is a point Burns himself makes in *Reviving the Strike*.

a broad community-teacher coalition to fight back and defend the interests of both—an opening, in other words, to create a true movement against free market education reform.

Repeatedly, the old leadership refused to work toward such a movement—so rank-and-file teachers created their own, working side by side with parents and students to fight back, eventually leading to the creation of CORE. That is, CORE originated as a group working not simply to push for better salaries or health-care coverage for teachers but to advance a broad vision of educational equality.

Other unions have struck in the wake of the CTU strike—some undoubtedly in part because of the example set by Chicago teachers. While some have claimed victory, others have unquestionably failed. The New York City public school bus drivers' strike of January 2013, examined at length in an important essay by Megan Erickson,[9] is an example of the perils posed when public sector unions simply walk off the job without a long-term strategy of movement building with working-class users of public services. Much like that of the Chicago teachers, the struggle of the New York school bus drivers could have been framed around the needs of both parents and community members whose children ride the buses as well as those of the drivers. A strike could have been a focal point around which both converged, with parents understanding—after a long-term campaign to build relationships with drivers—that the strike would be the means

---

9   Megan Erickson, "The Strike That Didn't Change New York," *Jacobin*, Spring 2013.

by which the union would fight for both better services for students and a more stable existence for drivers.

But while the union, Amalgamated Transit Union Local 1181, was willing to take the rare step of a strike, the union built no such movement. So when Mayor Michael Bloomberg and Education Chancellor Dennis Walcott both referred to the strike on separate occasions as "a strike against our children," there were no long-standing relationships between union members and parents that could insist on the contrary.[10] The strike was a failure.

Contrast this with the Chicago teachers strike. Mayor Emanuel, predictably, attempted to demonize teachers in similar ways, stating the day before the strike that "our kids do not deserve this." But during the strike, multiple polls showed that Emanuel's antistrike rhetoric fell on deaf ears: CPS parents backed the union over the mayor by huge majorities. As this book goes to press, those numbers still stand.[11]

The CTU strike shows that strikes are still labor's most powerful weapon. But they cannot lead to victory for labor—particularly in industries like education, transportation for children, and other sectors involving "care work"—by simply halting work without having those who depend on that labor on their side. Labor's opponents depend on their ability to malign organized workers by claiming that they are acting selfishly, without regard to the

10 Ibid.
11 Bob Sector and Rick Pearson, "Dim View on Emanuel Education Policy, Tribune Poll Finds," *Chicago Tribune*, May 22, 2013.

harm their actions will cause to the communities who depend on them. But because the teachers organized closely in those communities for years before their strike—with genuine empathy for community concerns and a willingness to shift focus and tactics on the basis of those communities' wishes—those accusations rang hollow when the strike came.[12]

The UPC, the union's old guard who maintained power for decades and would not fight—either by itself or with organized community groups—against the board's neoliberal agenda, did not disappear during CORE's tenure. They reappeared in 2013 at the head of a coalition of caucuses, the Coalition to Save Our Union (CSOU), within the CTU—a coalition that included ProActive Chicago Teachers (PACT), the liberal reform caucus that held power for one term in 2001. PACT moved from a union agitator for reform throughout the 1990s and 2000s into partnership with the forces that sought to roll back the gains won and the movement built by CORE. The coalition's platform focuses on losses around bread-and-butter issues in the contract negotiated during the 2012 strike, like pay, benefits, and the cost of health care.

The UPC's repeated inaction on school closures and refusal to work alongside community groups were among the principal reasons for CORE's initial formation, along with its

---

12   See JOMO, "Caring On Stolen Time: A Nursing Home Diary," *Dissent*, Winter 2013; Sarah Jaffe, "A Day Without Care," *Jacobin*, Spring 2013.

inability or unwillingness to take the union out on strike for a quarter century. But the CSOU tried to run to the left of CORE on school closures and the strike, claiming that the union's leadership should have stayed on strike until they won a moratorium on school closures. The union, the CSOU also argued, should focus more on servicing its members than forming a movement.

Chicago teachers had little interest in retreating from the broad movement they had helped to build; and CORE was decisively reelected, winning 79 percent of teachers' votes to the coalition's 21 percent.[13]

It is clear, then, that the CTU's agenda of left unionism is not being foisted on an unwilling or apathetic membership. Having seen what social movement unionism was capable of achieving, an overwhelming majority of Chicago's educators opted to go on trying to beat back an education policy of austerity in Chicago and the United States as a whole.

This huge level of interest in militant, democratic unionism on the part of educators themselves is what is required for the CTU or any union to mount an effective challenge to neoliberal education reform and neoliberal policies generally. Union leaders with strong left politics but an inability to educate and politicize their members will not be able to create a groundswell of resistance at workplaces and within communities—and will likely be hounded by those within the union who would rather focus on advancing members'

---

13 Micah Uetricht, "Chicago Teachers Union Overwhelmingly Re-Elects Karen Lewis's CORE Caucus," *The Nation*, May 20, 2013.

self-interests alone.[14] If community-union coalitions are going to be able to fight austerity, they will need to inspire the kind of widespread consciousness-raising at the rank-and-file level that has been seen within the CTU.

For at least another term, the CTU will continue to pursue a broad progressive agenda and help lead a city-wide movement for educational justice. But the poststrike maneuverings of the city's Board of Education (and the union's inability to halt them) are continuing. In particular, these efforts involve the closing of forty-nine public elementary schools and one high school program, almost entirely on the city's South and West sides in black neighborhoods in 2013, and a recent round of budget cuts that have totaled $162 million as well as mass teacher layoffs. All of these defeats raise the question of whether the kind of unionism that led to victory in the 2012 strike will be enough to halt the continued dismantlement of public education.

Shortly after the union's victory in the strike, the Board of Education announced its plans to shut down a massive number of public schools. It had already closed 110 schools since the late 1990s, usually a few each year. The board initially claimed that it had its sights on over 300 schools to be closed in 2013 alone; later, it shifted that number to some 130;

---

14   The failed attempts by New York City public transit workers to reform their union, Transit Workers Local 100, provide a strong case study, particularly for public sector workers. See Steve Downs, *Hell on Wheels: The Success and Failure of Reform in Transport Workers Union Local 100*, Against the Current, 2008.

finally, fifty schools were closed—the largest mass school closing in American history.

The justification for the closings has shifted wildly in short periods of time, oscillating in response to changing political winds or the exposure of one rationale as being dishonest or simply false: initially, schools were described as "failing" and therefore had to be shut down; after teachers and communities pushed back on this label, the justification became about an "underutilization crisis" and the efficient use of the district's scarce resources. Since the district's finances are scarce (the CPS board claims that it is facing a $1 billion budget deficit over the next three years), money has to be allocated efficiently—and this means the closing down of schools it claims are underutilized.

All of the board's justifications for these closures were repeatedly dismantled both by activists and the mainstream media. The board initially claimed, for example, that schools were massively underutilized because 145,000 school-age children had left the city over the previous decade; reporters quickly pointed out that the district's own numbers showed that less than 29,000 students had left the district during that time.[15] In schools it planned to close, the district cited huge percentages of underutilized classrooms, claiming that 140 schools were half-empty; independent analysis soon pointed out that the board's numbers were deeply flawed, based on

---

15   Linda Lutton and Becky Vevea, "Truth Squad: Enrollment Down in CPS, but Not By Much," WBEZ, December 10, 2012; Becky Vevea and Linda Lutton, "Fact Check: Chicago School Closings," WBEZ, May 16, 2013.

packing classrooms with as many as thirty-six students,
counting special education classrooms with fifteen students as
severely underutilized, and other dishonest statistical maneuverings.[16] The district initially claimed it would save $560
million by closing schools, but the board was soon forced to
admit that even with optimistic cost projections, it had exag-
gerated those costs significantly; the district also had not
included the over $200 million in loans to improve receiving
schools and the $25 million annual cost of servicing those
loans.[17] And while it was claimed that the closures were about
creating better education opportunities for students and that
all students whose schools closed would attend better-
performing schools, investigations by mainstream media
outlets quickly found this to be false, with both of the city's
major dailies reporting that around two thirds of students at
slated closures would now attend schools that, according to
district metrics, performed no better than their old schools.[18]

16   "On Space Utilization and the Narrative of Right-Sizing the District,"
Raise Your Hand for Illinois, ilraiseyourhand.org. The Illinois state maximum
class size for children with mild disabilities is fifteen or fewer students without a
paraprofessional, seventeen students with a paraprofessional. For students with
severe disabilities, the limit is eight without a parapro, thirteen with a parapro.
CPS calculations of underutilization treated all of these classrooms with disabled
students as underutilized. See Rebecca Harris, "Class Sizes Could Increase for
Special Education Students," *Catalyst Chicago*, February 27, 2013.
17   Linda Lutton, "'Zero Trust' After CPS Admits It Overstated
Savings from Closing Schools," WBEZ, May 6, 2013; Linda Lutton, "CPS
Will Go Further Into Debt to Pay for Upgrades at Receiving Schools,"
WBEZ, April 12, 2013.
18   Noreen S. Ahmed-Ullah, Jeff Coen, and Alex Richards, "Chicago
School Closings: A Closer Look at CPS Strategy," *Chicago Tribune*, April
12, 2013; Lauren Fitzpatrick and Art Golba, "Despite Promise, Not All
Schools on CPS Closing List Are Sending Kids to Schools with Better
Scores," *Chicago Sun-Times*, March 22, 2013.

As with so much of public policy governing public goods in the age of austerity, Chicago school closures are designed not to strengthen public education, but to dismantle it.

Closures are an example of what education scholar Pauline Lipman has described as the neoliberal state's "intervention . . . on the side of capital, first to destroy existing institutional arrangements, and then to create a new infrastructure for capital accumulation."[19] Public schools are shuttered under the guise of crisis and then immediately replaced by charter schools—often in the same buildings the public schools once inhabited: Some 40 percent of public schools closed since 2002 are now being run by private operators. Those charters then conduct aggressive outreach campaigns to draw students away from neighborhood schools that still exist, leading to additional empty seats in those schools, which are then labeled as underutilized. The district speaks of an "underutilization crisis" justifying its need to close 100 schools, yet it plans to open sixty new charters to accommodate 50,000 students.

The same spirit seen during the strike was rallied against school closings: In November 2012, teachers and community activists staged a sit-in on the fifth floor of City Hall, outside the mayor's office, demanding a moratorium on school closures and resulting in eleven arrests; the weekend before the final closings vote in May 2013, the union led a three-day march to all fifty-four schools slated for closure

---

19   Pauline Lipman, *The New Political Economy of Urban Education: Neoliberalism, Race, and the Right to the City*, Routledge, 2011, p. 29.

(four schools were removed at the eleventh hour); high school students whose schools were not being closed led multiple walkouts to protest the closings; City Hall and the Board of Education saw unannounced civil disobedience actions from teachers and activists in the week before the closure vote; protesting parents and teachers were dragged out of the Board of Education's meeting to vote on the final list of closures. At one point, inside of a South Side elementary, parents confronted a logistics firm hired to inventory the school before its "turnaround," actually knocking books out of staffers' hands and guarding the school's computers and other items in a classroom to prevent the firm from continuing its work.[20] Public opinion polls found, as they did during the strike, that a strong majority of Chicagoans backed the CTU and opposed Emanuel's plans.[21]

But teachers did not have the kind of leverage over the board that they had during the strike. And Mayor Emanuel likely saw the closure battle as one he could not afford to lose. The closures will likely cause upheaval to CPS students and their families, further devastation to communities that have long borne the brunt of disinvestment, and the loss of thousands of jobs for members of the CTU and other unions.

The closures targeted the South and West sides of the city, but a decision to shift the way the district funded schools led to budget cuts so massive that the district could no longer

---

20   Linda Lutton, "Parents at School Slated for Turnaround Chase Away CPS Inventory Team," WBEZ, April 25, 2013.
21   Bob Secter and Rick Pearson, "Dim View on Emanuel Education Policy, Tribune Poll Finds," *Chicago Tribune*, May 11, 2013.

meet meet the schools' most fundamental needs, such as providing supplies of toilet paper. CPS decided to shift the way it funded schools from granting block amounts for a given number of teaching positions to allocating money on a "per-pupil" basis (a move advocated by the Broad Foundation, one of the principal foundations pushing free market education reform).

The result was $162 million in budget cuts and 3,168 layoffs, including about 1,700 teachers. While many of those teachers were rehired, the classroom-level cuts have left many principals unable to meet the basic provisions legally mandated by the teachers union contract, like keeping class sizes below twenty-eight for elementary schools and thirty-one for middle and high schools. At the beginning of the 2013 school year, many teachers reported class sizes topping forty. Arts and physical education teachers and librarians, which many public schools never had to begin with, have been laid off in disproportionate numbers. Principals report that they will likely be forced to lay off veteran teachers because they cannot afford them—not as a one-off act but for as long as per-pupil budgeting remains in place. This will continue because principals will be forced to staff classrooms with a set amount of money and will be unable to justify hiring and keeping more experienced (and more expensive) teachers.[22]

The CTU fought both school closures and the shift to per-pupil funding, and it lost on both fronts. The implications of

---

22   Micah Uetricht, "New School Year Brings Anxiety for Chicago Parents," Al Jazeera America, August 23, 2013.

those defeats are fairly uncomfortable: Despite organizing at the community and rank-and-file levels, taking on the mayor and the Board of Education and the free market reformers, filing lawsuits and taking over public hearings, leading mass marches and civil disobedience actions, and winning the hearts and minds of a strong majority of the Chicago public, the CTU suffered stinging defeats. No matter how well-organized communities and workers are, the overwhelming power of free market forces and their representatives in public office may still triumph.

Still, in the fight against closures, the union strengthened its broad coalition with the community and other unions. And that coalition, along with the union's strike and general antagonism toward the neoliberal wing of the Democrats since 2010, has successfully created a political crisis in a city long accustomed to political stasis. School closures have opened up a rare space in the city council for members to break as a bloc, albeit tepidly, with the mayor. A progressive coalition has emerged within the council, speaking out against the school closings and lending its weight to other union and community fights; calls for Toni Preckwinkle, the somewhat progressive president of the Cook County Board, have gone up from newspaper columnists and grass-roots groups.

The CTU has announced plans to wade into city politics. The union has announced that it will register 100,000 new voters in the city, ostensibly in an attempt to take on Mayor Emanuel and other city council members backing him. The union's contract expires in 2015—timing that could create another political crisis for Emanuel should the union again turn contract negotiations into a pitched battle over Emanuel's education policies. And such a battle could help unseat him if a strong progressive candidate were to run. (In response to a media report about Emanuel's massive war chest, the union's political director Stacy Davis Gates told a Chicago newspaper, "He's going to need every damn dime.")[23]

There have also been rumblings of rank-and-file teachers running for city council and other positions in the city. As this book goes to press, the union continues to debate its course of action internally, with organizers aware of the conservatizing effect that electoral politics often has on social movements. But the feeling is that the union has no choice but to attempt to unseat the mayor and his political allies if public education is to be maintained in Chicago.

This shift to electoral politics is necessary because of the highly undemocratic ways in which education policy is currently crafted in Chicago. Like other large American cities undergoing free market education reform, including Washington, DC, and New York, Chicago's school board and CEO are appointed by the mayor and are thus completely unaccountable to the city's residents. During the battle over school closures, the union and community groups ran a months-long campaign utilizing a wide array of tactics to convince the Board of Education not to close the slated fifty-four schools; in the end, the unelected board, accountable

23 Natasha Korecki, "Chicago Teachers Union on Rahm $5 million: 'He Needs Every Damn Dime,'" *Chicago Sun-Times*, October 11, 2013.

only to the mayor and his wishes, closed fifty. If other mass closings or similarly devastating policies are to be avoided, legislative shifts will be necessary. And if the kind of internal democracy and militancy that have characterized CORE's governance of the union are to be maintained, the CTU will have to wade into electoral politics very carefully.

The CTU will have many opportunities to fail in the near future, and it will likely continue to lose some key battles. But the memory of CORE will continue to serve as an example of how the rank and file can push back against austerity and the union's own calcified leadership.

On the first day of the strike, after the entire city of Chicago had been blanketed by striking teachers, the teachers held a massive march in the city's downtown—the first of several throughout the walkout. I arrived as the march got under way. Entering in the middle of the crowd, I spent about fifteen minutes wading through the crush of people trying to get to the front, but I never found it. I jumped up on a concrete planter to try to see the march's end, but couldn't see that either.

We still see a few strikes in twenty-first-century America, but there is a palpable sense of desperation clinging to most of them. Battles may be won, but the outcome of the larger war between the working class and capital has long seemed settled. Still, as Chicago's education workers finished their first day on strike with a mass rally, I looked around. Tens of thousands of teachers, clinicians, and paraprofessionals were decked out in red, holding homemade signs decrying the

Board of Education or the mayor; some held signs with one hand and pushed strollers or tugged small children along. Many had never been to a rally before, but here they were, on strike, radiating a mixture of defiance and exhilaration.

As the march began to end, teachers took their time leaving the streets. They clearly enjoyed their sense of ownership over the city, shutting down large swaths of downtown at rush hour while everyone from McDonald's employees to suit-and-tie office workers yelled or gestured in solidarity.

Standing in the middle of a city where striking teachers could be seen every few blocks, where average passers-by spontaneously shouted out their support, where a struggle against neoliberal reform was center stage for weeks and was overwhelmingly supported by the city's residents, it became clear that the war had not yet ended. Maybe the working class could actually win.

A naïve thought, perhaps. But just a few years earlier, many felt that a small group of dissidents were naïve in thinking that they could win control of their union; a few months earlier, many Chicagoans thought it impossible that the union could ever achieve a strike after the newly restrictive legislation leveled against them; many observers thought it unlikely that a free market agenda on education backed by both political parties could be rolled back. And it wasn't long ago that those who dared to argue that the global neoliberal project was not the "end of history" were seen as naïve.

The CTU serves as a reminder that history—of education reform, of public sector unions, of the fight against austerity and the future of the working class—remains unwritten.